CLASSES
in MODERN
SOCIETY

T. B. Bottomore

*Department of Political Science, Sociology and
Anthropology, Simon Fraser University, Canada*

CLASSES
in MODERN
SOCIETY

VINTAGE BOOKS

A Division of Random House

New York

Contents

CLASSES
in MODERN
SOCIETY

I

INTRODUCTION

THE DIVISION of society into classes or strata, which are ranged in a hierarchy of wealth, prestige and power, is a prominent and almost universal feature of social structure which has always attracted the attention of social theorists and philosophers. During the greater part of human history this inequality among men has been generally accepted as an unalterable fact. Ancient and medieval writers, when they touched upon the subject of the social hierarchy, always tended to provide a rationalization and justification of the established order, very often in terms of a religious doctrine concerning the origin of social ranks. This is most apparent, perhaps, in the Hindu religious myths about the formation of the caste system. On the other side, the sporadic rebellions of the poor and oppressed were usually revolts against particularly irksome conditions rather than against the whole system of ranks, and they did not give rise to any clear conceptions of an alternative form of society.

Only in modern times, and particularly since the American and French Revolutions, has social class, as a stark embodiment of the principle of inequality, become an object of scientific study, and at the same time of widespread condemnation in terms of new social doctrines. The revolutionary ideal of equality, however variously it was interpreted by nineteenth-century thinkers, at least implied an opposition to hereditary privileges and to an immutable hierarchy of ranks. The revolutions of the late eighteenth century and the early nineteenth century, directed against the legal and political privileges which survived from the system of feudal estates, brought about an extension of civil and political rights and a greater degree of equality of opportunity. But at the same time they created a new social hierarchy, based directly upon the possession of wealth, and this in turn came to be attacked during the nineteenth century by socialist thinkers who believed that the ideal of equality ultimately implied a "classless society."

During the past hundred years great changes have taken place in the social structure of the advanced industrial countries. The history of this period can be seen in part as a record of the growth of equality in new spheres of social life, or as some writers have expressed

it, of the growth of citizenship.[1] *Laissez-faire* capitalism
—and especially the doctrine of *laissez faire*, which was
far more extreme than the practice—has more or less
vanished; and in all the industrial countries there is
some degree of central economic planning, some attempt to regulate the distribution of wealth and income,
and a more or less elaborate public provision of a wide
range of social services. But there are important differences between the two principal types of industrial
societies, the Western capitalist societies[2] and the
Soviet-type societies of Eastern Europe. In the former,
there has been a gradual and limited movement towards
"classlessness," which is usually held to be especially
marked in the past two decades—the era of the Welfare State—and which has resulted from changes in
the relative earnings of different occupational groups
and in rates of taxation, improvements in education and
social services, increasing opportunities for individual

[1] See especially T. H. Marshall, *Citizenship and Social Class* (London, 1950).

[2] I use the terms "capitalism" and "capitalist society" as they are
habitually used by economic historians and sociologists, to refer to an
economic and social system existing during a particular historical
period, which is characterized principally by freedom of the market,
free labour (i.e. individuals who are legally free and economically
compelled to sell their labour power on the market), and private
ownership of the means of production by industrial enterprises. These,
together with secondary characteristics, make it possible to distinguish
with reasonable clarity between capitalism and other types of society,
such as feudalism or socialist society. This is not to say, however, that
actual capitalist societies have remained unchanged since their origins,
that there are not subtypes of capitalism, or that mixed and transitional
forms of society cannot occur. Some of these problems will be discussed more fully later in this book.

social mobility, and perhaps most of all, from the recent rapid growth in total national income. These changes will be examined more closely in a later chapter, but it is clear at once that they do not amount to an abolition of social classes. The Western societies are still capitalist, in the sense that their economic systems are dominated by privately owned industrial enterprises and that very pronounced social differences exist between the group of industrial property-owners and the group of wage-earners.

In the Soviet-type societies, on the other hand, the claim is made that social classes, or at least the hierarchical class structure, have disappeared with the abolition of private ownership of the means of production; and that the construction of a classless, socialist society is under way. This claim was not at first very closely examined, even by the critics of Soviet society, who concentrated their attention, during the Stalinist period, upon more blatant features of the social system—the repression of personal freedom and the prevalence of coercion and terror. Indeed, it seems to have been quite widely held at one time that the political dictatorship itself could be explained—in terms of an antithesis between liberty and equality—as a consequence of the attempt to enforce an unnatural equality of condition upon the members of society. But this was seen to be implausible when it was realized that there were great social inequalities in the Soviet-type societies; and in more recent studies the discussion has centred upon the emergence of a "new ruling class" in these societies, and upon comparisons between the characteristics of elite groups in the Western and Soviet societies.

It is the main purpose of this book to consider how the movement towards social equality which began with the eighteenth-century revolutions has affected the social hierarchy in the industrial societies, and how, in turn, it has been influenced by the development of modern industry. This calls, in the first place, for an inquiry into the nature of modern social classes. It requires, secondly, a comparative study of the changes in social stratification which have occurred in the two principal types of industrial society, and an attempt to explain these changes. Lastly, it involves a confrontation between the ideas of equality and social hierarchy. Is equality an attainable ideal in the circumstances of a complex industrial society? And conversely, what kinds and degrees of inequality are inescapable, tolerable, or even desirable, in such a society?

The inequalities of social class should not be regarded as identical with human inequality in general. There are other forms of inequality, other kinds of privilege and domination, besides those which arise from differences of social class. Within particular societies there may be inequalities originating in differences of race, language or religion; and between societies there exist inequalities such as those so evident today between rich and poor nations, which are the outcome of conquest, of differences in size and natural resources, and of specific historical opportunities and failures. Nor are political rights always determined by class membership, as Marxists sometimes assert. Political power itself may create new social classes, new property rights, new privileges.

It remains true, none the less, that the division of society into distinct social classes is one of the most striking manifestations of inequality in the modern world, that it has often been the source of other kinds of inequality, and that the economic dominance of a particular class has very often been the basis for its political rule. Class, therefore, is deeply involved in many of the most vital questions of modern politics and social policy.

I I

THE NATURE
OF SOCIAL CLASS

THERE IS still much controversy among sociologists about the theory of social class, and more broadly, of social stratification. The latter term may be used to refer to any hierarchical ordering of social groups or strata in a society; and sociologists have generally distinguished its principal forms as being those of caste, estate, social class, and status group. Each of these types of social stratification is complex, and there are many unsettled questions about the basis and characteristics of castes and estates, just as there are about classes and status groups[1]; even though the former are more easily defined, and their boundaries more clearly distinguishable, in

[1] See, for an excellent review of recent studies of caste, M. N. Srinivas *et al.*, "Caste," *Current Sociology*, VIII (3) 1959; and on the social hierarchy in feudal societies, Marc Bloch, *Feudal Society* (English trans., Chicago, 1961), Part VI.

most cases. In spite of these difficulties, there are some general features of social stratification which are not in dispute.

In the first place, a system of ranks does not form part of some natural and invariable order of things, but is a human contrivance or product, and is subject to historical changes. More particularly, natural or biological inequalities, on one side, and the distinctions of social rank on the other, belong to two distinct orders of fact. The differences were pointed out very clearly by Rousseau in a well-known passage: "I conceive that there are two kinds of inequality among the human species; one, which I call natural or physical, because it is established by nature, and consists in a difference of age, health, bodily strength, and the qualities of the mind or of the soul; and another, which may be called moral or political inequality, because it depends on a kind of convention, and is established, or at least authorized, by the consent of men. This latter consists of the different privileges, which some men enjoy to the prejudice of others; such as that of being more rich, more honoured, more powerful, or even in a position to exact obedience."[2]

The distinction has been recognized by most modern writers on social class. Thus T. H. Marshall has observed that "the institution of class teaches the members of a society to notice some differences and to ignore others when arranging persons in order of social merit."[3] It might be argued, however, while accepting this distinc-

[2] J. J. Rousseau, *A Dissertation on the Origin and Foundation of the Inequality of Mankind,* Everyman edition, p. 160.

[3] T. H. Marshall, "The Nature of Class Conflict" in *Citizenship and Social Class* (London, 1950), p. 115.

tion, that the social-class system in modern capitalist societies does actually operate in such a way as to ensure a rough correspondence between the hierarchy of natural abilities and the socially recognized distinctions of rank. Such arguments have often been put forward,[4] but they are not well supported by the facts. It is generally admitted that the inequality of incomes is one important element in the class hierarchy. But numerous investigations have established that the inequality of incomes depends very largely upon the unequal distribution of property through inheritance, and not primarily upon the differences in earned income which might be supposed to have some connection with natural, or innate, abilities.[5] Modern studies of educational and occupational selection underline this lack of correspondence between the hierarchies of ability and of social position, inasmuch as they make clear that intellectual ability, for example, is by no means always rewarded with high income or high social status, nor lack of ability with the opposite. Indeed, it would be a more accurate description of the social-class system to say that it operates, largely through the inheritance of property, to ensure that each individual maintains a certain social position, determined by his birth and irrespective of his particular abilities. This state of affairs is only mitigated, not abolished, by various social influences which we shall consider later.

[4] They are to be found especially in the elite theories of Pareto and Mosca which I have criticized in my *Elites and Society* (New York, 1965).

[5] See, for instance, Hugh Dalton, *Some Aspects of the Inequality of Incomes in Modern Societies* (New York, 1920).

A second point of general agreement is that social classes, in contrast with castes or feudal estates, are more exclusively economic groups. They are not constituted or supported by any specific legal or religious rules, and membership in a particular class confers upon the individual no special civil or political rights. It follows from this that the boundaries of social classes are less precisely defined. The principal classes, the *bourgeoisie* and the working class, may be fairly easily identifiable in most societies, but there are many intermediate strata, conveniently referred to as the "middle classes," the boundaries of which are difficult to state exactly, and membership in which cannot be determined in any simple fashion.

Furthermore, the membership of modern social classes is usually less stable than that of other types of hierarchical group. The individual is born into a particular social class, just as he is born into a caste or estate, but he is somewhat less likely to remain at the social level in which he was born than is the individual in a caste or estate society. Within his own lifetime an individual, or his family, may rise or fall in the social hierarchy. If he rises, he needs no patent of nobility, no kind of official recognition, to confirm his new status. It will be enough for him to be wealthy, to have a particular economic and occupational role, and perhaps to acquire some of the secondary cultural characteristics of the social stratum into which he has moved.

Although the economic basis of social classes is obvious, the fact may be interpreted in various ways, which give rise to widely differing views of the significance of classes in social life and of the relations between classes. It will be useful to begin by examining Marx's interpretation, because it affirms so strongly the economic basis of classes and the antagonistic relations between them, and because a critical study of Marx's conception will reveal most of the vital problems concerning the nature of social classes.

Marx never set down a full and systematic account of his theory of class, although it may reasonably be said (as Lenin remarked) that everything he wrote was in some way concerned with the question of class. The point at which Marx began a connected exposition of his theory is just where the manuscript of the third volume of *Capital* breaks off unfinished, after one page in which he had set out mainly the difficulties which confronted his own theory. In fact, Marx first of all adopted a notion of class which was widely employed by historians and social theorists (including the early socialists) at the time when he began his sociological inquiries, and he was then largely concerned to fit this notion into the wider framework of his theory of social change, and to use it in analysing the development of one particular social system, namely modern capitalism. He indicated this himself when he wrote, in an early letter, "no credit is due to me for discovering the existence of classes in modern society, nor yet the struggle between them. Long before me bourgeois historians had described the historical development of this struggle of the classes and bourgeois economists the economic anatomy of the classes."[6] Marx went on to explain his own contribution as having been to show that the existence of classes is bound up with particular historical phases in the development of production, and that the conflict of classes in the modern capitalist societies will lead to the victory of the working class and to the inauguration of a classless, socialist society.

The distinctive features of Marx's theory are, therefore, the conception of social classes in terms of the system of production, and the idea of social development through class conflict which is to culminate in a new type of society without classes. As Marx saw it, "the whole of what is called world history is nothing but the creation of man himself by human labour."[7] Man produces (and reproduces) himself in a physical and in a cultural sense. "In the social production which men carry on, they enter into definite relations that are indispensable and independent of their will; these relations of production correspond to a definite stage of development of their material powers of production. The totality of these relations of production constitutes the economic structure of society—the real foundation upon which legal and political superstructures arise and to which definite forms of social consciousness correspond. The mode of production of material life determines the general character of the social, political and spiritual processes of life."[8]

[6] Letter to J. Weydemeyer, March 5, 1852.
[7] *Economic and Philosophical Manuscripts* (1844).
[8] *Contribution to the Critique of Political Economy* (1859). Preface.

[14]

Social classes originated with the first historical expansion of productive forces beyond the level needed for mere subsistence, involving the extension of the division of labour outside the family, the accumulation of surplus wealth, and the emergence of private ownership of economic resources. Thereafter, it is the differing relations of individuals to the privately owned instruments of production which form the basis for the constitution of social classes. Marx distinguished several important epochs, or major forms of social structure, in the history of mankind. In the preface to his *Contribution to the Critique of Political Economy* he writes: "In broad outline we can designate the Asiatic, the ancient, the feudal, and the modern bourgeois modes of production as epochs in the progress of the economic formation of society." Elsewhere, he and Engels refer to primitive communism, ancient society (slavery), feudal society (serfdom), and modern capitalism (wage labour) as the principal historical forms of society. Marx's references to the Asiatic type of society are especially interesting because this lies outside the line of development of the Western societies, and also because he seems to accept the possibility that in this case a ruling class might be formed by the high officials who control the administration.[9] But this theme was not pursued in his later work.

[9] See, on this question, the interesting essay by George Lichtheim, "Marx and the 'Asiatic Mode of Production,'" *Far Eastern Affairs*, No. 3 (St. Anthony's Papers No. 14; Carbondale, Ill., 1963). See also Marx's observations on pre-capitalist societies, taken from his preparatory manuscripts for *Capital*, in Karl Marx, *Pre-Capitalist Eco-*

The historical changes from one type of society to another are brought about by class struggles and by the victory of one class over others. Class conflict itself reflects the incompatibility between different modes of production; and the victory of a particular class, as well as its subsequent reorganization of society, is conditional upon the emergence of a new and superior mode of production, which it is the interest of this class to establish as dominant. In Marx's words: "No social order ever disappears before all the productive forces for which there is room in it have been developed; and new, higher relations of production never appear before the material conditions of their existence have matured in the womb of the old society."[10]

Marx was not, however, expounding a simple theory of technological or economic determinism. On the contrary, as he asserted in his criticism of Hegel's philosophy of history: "It is not 'history' which uses men as a means of achieving—as if it were an individual person—*its* own ends. History is *nothing* but the activity

---

nomic *Formations,* edited by E. J. Hobsbawm (Los Angeles, 1963). Hobsbawm, in his introduction, argues that these texts show that Marx was not attempting to set out a general evolutionary scheme; but while it may be accepted that Marx was not an evolutionist in the grand manner of Comte or Spencer, it is to exaggerate in the opposite direction to claim that he had no evolutionary scheme at all in mind. There are several problems which Marx failed to resolve clearly in his writings; and one of them is precisely the question whether the transition from feudalism to capitalism, and the develpment of capitalist society, were to be regarded as special cases, or whether, and in what manner, they could be incorporated in a general account of the development of human society from its beginnings.

[10] *Contribution to the Critique of Political Economy.* Preface.

of men in pursuit of their ends.[11] Marx held very strongly (and his own intellectual and political activities would otherwise have been absurd) that the victory of a rising class depends upon its awareness of its situation and aims, and upon the effectiveness of its political organization, as well as upon its actual economic position. This is especially the case with the working class in capitalist society, and Marx discussed on several occasions the factors which might influence the development of its class consciousness and of its political maturity. In *The Poverty of Philosophy*, for example, he examines at some length the development of the working class, and adds some critical remarks on the lack of empirical studies devoted to this most significant social movement: "Many researches have been undertaken to trace the historical stages through which the *bourgeoisie* passed, from the commune up to its constitution as a class. But when it is a question of gaining a clear understanding of the strikes, combinations, and other forms in which the proletarians are achieving, before our eyes, their organization as a class, some are seized with genuine fear, while others display a transcendental disdain." It is one of the most important features of Marx's theory of class, therefore, that it attempts to take account of the interplay between the real situation of individuals in the process of production, on one side, and the conceptions which they form of their situation and of the lines of social and political action which are open to them, on the other; and in its application to

[11] *The Holy Family* (1845).

modern societies the theory allows a very great influence to ideas and doctrines. Marx's conviction that the working class would be victorious within a relatively short space of time in its struggle against the *bourgeoisie* was founded largely upon his conclusion that modern large-scale factory production would be extremely favourable to the development of class consciousness, to the diffusion of socialist ideas, and to the organization of a political movement.

Like other nineteenth-century thinkers who contributed to the foundation of sociology, Marx was particularly concerned to investigate the origins and development of modern capitalist society, and he chose to do so largely in a single country—England—because it was at that time the most advanced industrial country, showing to others, as Marx claimed, "the image of their own future." In its application to this English society of the mid-nineteenth century Marx's theory was extremely convincing. The course of industrial development seemed to confirm the thesis that society was becoming more clearly divided into two principal classes, a small class of increasingly wealthy capitalists and a growing mass of propertyless and impoverished wage-earners; and that the social gulf between them was widening as a result of the decline of the middle classes (by which Marx meant the small independent producers and independent professional men), whose members were being transformed into dependent employees. At the same time, the rise of the labour movement (of trade unions, co-operatives, and socialist political parties) and the outbreak of revolutionary conflicts all over Europe, especially in the years preceding 1848, provided evidence for Marx's prediction of a growth of class consciousness in the working class, and its expression in new social doctrines and new forms of political organization.

For the past eighty years Marx's theory has been the object of unrelenting criticism and of tenacious defence. These have concerned themselves with three principal aspects of the theory. First, there is the criticism which questions the pre-eminence that Marx assigned to social classes and class conflicts in explaining the major historical changes in human society. As a result of his preoccupation with class, it is said, Marx neglected other important social relationships, and in particular those which bind men together in national communities. This distorted his account of social change in two ways. It led him to underestimate the influence of nationalism and of conflict between nations in human history; an excusable error, perhaps, in the mid-nineteenth century, when Comte and Spencer, for example, both considered that warfare was likely to disappear altogether from human affairs. The growth of nationalist and imperialist sentiments during the latter part of the nineteenth century constitutes a particular problem for Marx's own theory, for although it can be interpreted as a diffusion of ruling-class ideas the question remains as to why such ideas and sentiments were able to influence such a large part of the population at a time when the working-class movement was growing vigorously and when Marxist doctrines were already widely known.

Marx also took little account of another aspect of the

growing sense of national community in the European nations, which restrained and moderated the development of class antagonisms. In the mid-nineteenth century it was easy to distinguish the "two nations" within each society; one of them participating fully and actively in, and directing, national affairs, while the other constituted only the raw material of policy. It was easy, too, to discern the massive movement of revolt which was taking shape among the members of this submerged and oppressed "nation." Yet even in Marx's lifetime there had begun the extension of political and social rights to new groups in the population, which has continued more rapidly in the twentieth century, and which has altered the relations between classes. New moral and social conceptions which emphasize common human interests within the nation, and the idea of "citizenship," have been in part a cause, in part a consequence, of these changes.

The failure of class antagonisms in the industrial countries to attain that degree of intensity which Marx had anticipated, was shown most dramatically in 1914, when the European socialist parties, many of them Marxist in doctrine, supported almost unanimously the war waged by their own governments. The same phenomenon is, however, revealed in a less dramatic way by the changes in working-class politics during the twentieth century from revolutionary to reformist ideas and actions. In this process, it may be claimed, the social bond of nationality has proved more effective in creating a community than has that of class.

[20]

A second theme in the criticism of Marx has been that although his theory fits reasonably well the phenomena of class relations in modern capitalist societies, it does not fit so well, nor has it been used so successfully in explaining, a number of other types of social stratification. There are, in fact, in Marx's theory, two distinct uses of the term "class" which illustrate this difficulty.[12] Very often—as in the famous opening passage of the *Communist Manifesto*, which begins: "The history of all hitherto existing society is the history of class struggles"—Marx employs the term "class" to refer to the major social groups—oppressors and oppressed—which are in conflict with each other in every type of human society beyond the most primitive. Elsewhere, however, Marx recognizes the distinctive features of modern social classes. In *The German Ideology*, he contrasts a class system with a system of estates, and observes: "The distinction between the personal and the class individual, the accidental nature of conditions of life for the individual, appears only with the emergence of class, which itself is a product of the *bourgeoisie*." Marx devoted himself largely to studying "class" in this second sense, as his scientific works make abundantly clear, and so he did not have to confront in detail the difficulties which arise when his general theory of class is used to explain the origins and development of feudal societies, of a caste system, or of the Asiatic form of society

[12] The best account of the different conceptions of class which Marx brought together in his theory will be found in S. Ossowski, *Class Structure in the Social Consciousness* (New York, 1963), Chapter 5.

which he had himself distinguished and briefly portrayed. The criticism here is not that Marx himself failed to test his theory in a sufficiently comprehensive way. He had formulated a new and exciting hypothesis, and had sought to test it rigorously in the case which he considered most significant from a theoretical and practical point of view: namely, the development of modern capitalism. The failure is that of later Marxists, who have for the most part abstained from examining the usefulness and limitations of the theory when applied to other historical situations.

The third line of criticism, which most nearly concerns us here, attacks directly Marx's account of the development of social classes in the modern capitalist societies. In broad outline, Marx predicted that the social gulf between the two principal classes, *bourgeoisie* and proletariat, would become wider, in part because of the increasing disparity between their conditions of life,[13] and in part because of the elimination of the intermediate strata of the population; that the class consciousness of the proletariat would develop and would assume a revolutionary character; and that the rule of the *bourgeoisie* would finally be overthrown by a revolution of the immense majority of the population.

Against this view numerous arguments have been

[13] Contrary to a popular belief Marx did not assert that the material level of living of the working class must decline absolutely with the development of capitalism; his principal argument was that it would decline relative to that of the *bourgeoisie*, either by remaining stationary while the latter rose, or by rising less rapidly. See his brief exposition in *Wage-Labour and Capital* (1848).

presented, based upon sociological observation of the changes in the structure of modern societies. It is claimed, in the first place, that the gulf between *bourgeoisie* and proletariat has not widened, for several reasons. The productivity of modern industry, especially in the last few decades, has increased so greatly as to produce a considerable improvement in the general level of living; and even if the distribution of income between the classes had remained unchanged this would still have raised the working-class level of living to a point at which new aspirations and new social attitudes would be encouraged, far removed from those which support revolutionary aims. It is argued further, however, that the distribution of national income has actually changed in favour of the working class, thus reinforcing these tendencies. The extent of the redistribution of income and wealth in modern societies is a subject of controversy, and some of the relevant studies will be considered in the next chapter; but even a modest redistribution, together with the general rise in incomes, the expansion of social services, and greater security of employment, would clearly bring about an important change in the position of the working class in society. It seems no longer possible in this second half of the twentieth century to regard the working class in the advanced industrial countries as being totally alienated from society, or, in Marx's phrase, as "a class *in* civil society which is not a class *of* civil society."

Another change which presents difficulties for Marx's theory is the growth of the "new middle classes." This does not directly falsify Marx's statement that the "middle classes" would gradually disappear in modern societies, because he was referring to the large numbers of small producers, craftsmen, artisans, small farmers, self-employed professional men, many of whom have in fact been absorbed as paid employees into large capitalist enterprises. Nevertheless, it does contradict one of Marx's fundamental arguments, which was that the "intermediate strata" would disappear, and that a simplified class structure of two clearly defined major classes would emerge. In the *Communist Manifesto* he wrote: "Our epoch, the epoch of *bourgeoisie,* possesses, however, this distinctive feature; it has simplified the class antagonisms. Society as a whole is more and more splitting up into two great hostile camps, into two great classes directly facing each other—*bourgeoisie* and proletariat."

The growth of the new middle classes—comprising office workers, supervisors, managers, technicians, scientists, and many of those who are employed in providing services of one kind or another (e.g. social welfare, entertainment, leisure activities)—which has resulted from economic development, manifests the greater complexity of social stratification in modern industrial societies, and it introduces, or reintroduces, as an important element of stratification, social prestige based upon occupation, consumption and style of life. Max Weber, who was the first to present a comprehensive alternative to Marx's theory, did so by distinguishing, in the first place, between different modes of stratification which coexisted in modern societies: class stratification, with which Marx had been primarily concerned, and stratification by social prestige or honour. He also treated as an independent phenomenon the distribution of political power in society, which Marx had viewed almost exclusively as the product of class stratification. In Weber's conception it is clear that stratification by prestige, which gives rise to the formation of status groups, is regarded as having its source in those pre-capitalist groups which enjoyed social honour, such as the various sections of the nobility, the scholarly professions, and the high officials; but the new middle classes in the advanced industrial societies exhibit some at least of the same features in basing their claims to social position upon educational and cultural characteristics, upon the nature of their occupations, and upon their particular styles of life.

Stratification by prestige affects the class system, as Marx conceived it, in two important ways: first, by interposing between the two major classes a range of status groups which bridge the gulf between the extreme positions in the class structure; and secondly, by suggesting an entirely different conception of the social hierarchy as a whole, according to which it appears as a continuum of more or less clearly defined status positions, determined by a variety of factors and not simply by property ownership, which is incompatible with the formation of massive social classes and with the existence of a fundamental conflict between classes. The relations between status groups at different levels are relations of competition and emulation, not of conflict. With the growth in numbers of the middle classes, which form an increasing proportion of the whole population, this view of the social hierarchy as a continuum of prestige ranks (or statuses) without any sharp breaks, and thus without any clear lines of conflict between major social groups, has acquired a much greater influence upon social thought, and its diffusion has served to check the growth of class consciousness. Consequently, whereas Max Weber regarded class stratification and status stratification as coexisting in modern societies, their relative importance fluctuating with changes in technology and economic conditions, some recent sociologists have concluded that status groups have now become far more important than social classes in the system of stratification as a whole.

This conclusion is supported by two other arguments. One of them asserts that the amount of social mobility in industrial societies is so considerable as to prevent the consolidation and persistence of classes in Marx's sense, and that, on the contrary, it too makes plausible the image of the social hierarchy as a series of levels of prestige, as a ladder with closely adjacent rungs, which individuals may climb or descend according to their capacities.[14] However, the amount and range of social mobility, like the distribution of income, have been

[14] This view is implied in the functionalist theory of social stratification presented by K. Davis and W. E. Moore in their article "Some Principles of Stratification," *American Sociological Review*, April, 1945; and also, to some extent, in S. M. Lipset's and R. Bendix's *Social Mobility in Industrial Society* (Berkeley, 1959).

assessed in conflicting ways, and some of the evidence from recent studies will be considered later.

A second argument, which derives ultimately from Weber's distinction between class stratification and the distribution of political power, has been set out most forcefully by Ralf Dahrendorf, in his *Class and Class Conflict in Industrial Society.* Dahrendorf's main thesis is that the coincidence of economic conflict and political conflict, which was the foundation of Marx's theory, has ceased to exist in what he terms the "post-capitalist societies." In capitalist society, Dahrendorf argues, "the lines of industrial and political conflict were superimposed. The opponents of industry—capital and labour —met again, as *bourgeoisie* and proletariat, in the political arena. . . . It is one of the central theses of the present analysis that in post-capitalist society, industry and society have, by contrast to capitalist society, been dissociated. Increasingly, the social relations of industry, including industrial conflict, do not dominate the whole of society but remain confined in their patterns and problems to the sphere of industry. Industry and industrial conflict are, in post-capitalist society, institutionally isolated, i.e. confined within the borders of their proper realm and robbed of their influence on other spheres of society" (op. cit., p. 268). Considered empirically, however, these propositions are more easily falsified than those of Marx which they are intended to replace; for numerous studies have shown that in the European industrial countries, and to a lesser extent in the USA, the major political conflicts are closely and continuously associated with industrial conflicts, and express the divergent interests of the principal social classes. Dahrendorf's criticisms of Marx's theory are more plausible in their less extreme formulations; as for example, that there are other conflict groups in society besides social classes, which may at times assume great importance, that the association between industrial conflict and political conflict cannot simply be taken for granted, but must be investigated in each case, and that, with the development of the capitalist industrial societies, some significant changes have occurred in the nature of political conflicts themselves which could not be clearly foreseen or taken into account by Marx.

Besides the kind of criticism we have just considered, which questions Marx's account of the relations between classes, there is another which disputes the validity of his analysis of the principal classes— *bourgeoisie* and proletariat—in view of the changes which they have undergone during the twentieth century. The *bourgeoisie*, it is argued, is no longer a closed, cohesive and enduring group. Its structure, its composition, and its stability over time have all been profoundly modified by the wider diffusion of property ownership and the breakup of large fortunes, by increasing social mobility, and by other changes in society. Furthermore, it can no longer be maintained that the *bourgeoisie* is a *ruling* class; first, because it has ceased to be a cohesive group; secondly, because the complexity and differentiation of modern societies make it difficult for any single group to wield power alone; and finally, because universal suffrage ensures that political power is ultimately in the hands of the mass of the people.

The changes in the condition of the working class appear even more damaging to Marx's theory. Marx expected the working class to become more homogeneous, because differences of skill and earnings would be reduced, if not obliterated, by the more extensive use of machinery; to become numerically stronger, because many members of the old middle class would sink to the condition of wage-earners; to become more united and class conscious as a result of the increasing similarity of conditions of life and work, the facility of communication among working-class organizations, and the spread of socialist doctrines; and finally, to become a revolutionary force, because of the growing disparity between its own material conditions and those of the *bourgeoisie*, and the realization that only a radical transformation of society could make possible a tolerable human life for the great majority of men. Against this conception, the critics have pointed out that the modern working class remains highly differentiated in respect of levels of skill, even though differences in earnings have tended to diminish; that increasing specialization of occupations has created a far more complex status system, as well as a multiplicity of sectional interests; that the expansion of the middle classes has reduced the proportion of industrial workers in the total population and thereby diminished their social influence; that greater social mobility has undermined the solidarity of the working class; and that the general improvement in levels of living has led to the *embourgeoisement* of the working class as a whole, which is now adopting middle-class standards and patterns of life.

Some part of this criticism has certainly to be accepted in any realistic account of the working class in present-day industrial societies, but the changes which have taken place are still open to various interpretations. The most disputed thesis is that concerning the *embourgeoisement* of the working class, which has often been presented in a superficial and facile manner. It has only recently been examined carefully by Goldthorpe and Lockwood,[15] who observe that as a result of recent studies of British society, "a picture has been built up—and it is one which would be generally accepted—of a system of stratification becoming increasingly fine in its gradations and at the same time somewhat less extreme and less rigid. Of late, however, still further economic progress has resulted in a new factor entering into the discussion—that of working class 'affluence.' . . . It has been argued by a number of writers that the working class, or at least a more prosperous section of it, is losing its identity as a social stratum and is becoming merged into the middle class. . . . This, one should note, is to claim a far more rapid and far-reaching change in class structure than any which could ensue from secular trends in occupational

[15] John H. Goldthorpe and David Lockwood, "Affluence and the British Class Structure," *The Sociological Review*, XI (2), July, 1963, pp. 133–63.

distribution, in the overall distribution of income and wealth or in rates of intergenerational social mobility." The authors then distinguish and examine what they call the economic, the relational and the normative aspects of the changes in working-class life. They point out that the economic progress of the working class in relation to the middle class has been exaggerated in many studies, because these do not take account of all the relevant factors, such as economic security, opportunities for promotion, and fringe benefits of various kinds. The other aspects, the relational (i.e. the extent to which manual workers are accepted on terms of equality by middle-class people in formal and informal social relationships) and the normative (i.e. the extent to which manual workers have acquired a new outlook and new standards of behaviour which resemble those of the middle class), have hardly been studied at all; but such evidence as there is suggests that the gulf between working class and middle class remains very wide. It follows that the political conclusions—the end of ideology and of class conflict— drawn from the so-called *embourgeoisement* of the working class, or in other words, from the view that the modern industrial countries are now middle-class societies, are themselves extremely dubious.

A recent French study, by Serge Mallet,[16] points to some conclusions which supplement those reached by Goldthorpe and Lockwood. Mallet makes an important distinction between the situation of the worker in the

[16] Serge Mallet, *La Nouvelle Classe ouvrière* (Paris, 1963).

spheres of consumption and of production. In the former, "the working class has ceased to live apart. Its level of living and its aspirations for material comfort have led it out of the ghetto in which it was confined at the beginning of industrialization. The worker ceases to regard himself as a worker when he leaves the factory." In the process of production itself, on the contrary, "the fundamental characteristics which distinguish the working class from other social strata seem to have remained unchanged."[17] It is in industry, through the factory organizations and the trade unions, that the distinctive characteristics and outlook of the working class are maintained or changed; and Mallet argues, from his studies of three industrial enterprises, that the "new working class" has been led, as a result of technological and economic changes, to assume greater responsibility for the organization of production, through its trade-union representatives, and thus to see itself still, and perhaps even more clearly, as the eventual controller of industry in place of the present capitalist owners.

We have lastly to consider a criticism of Marx's theory which arises directly from the social and political experiences of the Soviet-type countries. It is best expressed in the words of a Polish sociologist, the late Stanislaw Ossowski: "There are other reasons why the nineteenth-century conception of social class, in both the liberal and the Marxian interpretations, has lost much of its applicability in the modern world. In situa-

[17] Ibid., p. 9.

tions where changes of social structure are to a greater or lesser extent governed by the decision of the political authorities, we are a long way from social class as interpreted by Marx, Ward, Veblen or Weber, from classes conceived of as groups determined by their relations to the means of production or, as others would say, by their relations to the market. We are a long way from classes conceived of as groups arising out of the spontaneously created class organizations. In situations where the political authorities can overtly and effectively change the class structure; where the privileges that are most essential for social status, including that of a higher share in the national income, are conferred by a decision of the political authorities; where a large part or even the majority of the population is included in a stratification of the type to be found in a bureaucratic hierarchy—the nineteenth-century concept of class becomes more or less an anachronism, and class conflicts give way to other forms of social antagonism."[18] This is most clearly apposite to the USSR, and to societies of the same type, in which the rule of a single party, unchecked by any organized opposition, has allowed an authoritarian ordering of income and rank in a highly inegalitarian system; but it also has some relevance to the modern capitalist societies, in which the state has acquired a degree of independence from social classes and is now a source of changes in stratification through its own social legislation.

[18] S. Ossowski, *Class Structure in the Social Consciousness*, p. 184.

Neither of these instances can be comprehended by the Marxist theory in its most rigorous form. Marx did not foresee either that the dictatorship of the proletariat as he conceived it would actually appear as the dictatorship of a party, and eventually as a bureaucratic regime controlled by a single individual, or that in the capitalist countries the working-class movement itself would help to bring about a form of society, the Welfare State, which may be transitional or enduring, which is not socialist, but in which there is a substantial control by government over the economy and social conditions, and a corresponding influence upon the system of stratification.

The criticisms of Marx's theory, and the alternative views which have been put forward, based mainly upon Max Weber's distinction between class stratification and stratification by prestige, do not amount as yet to a comprehensive new theory, which can take the place of that which Marx proposed. They provide, rather, a more or less systematic inventory of the outstanding problems—the nature of social stratification in the Soviet societies, and of its modifications in the capitalist societies; the relative importance of property ownership, educational selection, occupational differentiation, and political power, in creating and maintaining social distinctions; the extent and consequences of social mobility and of income inequalities—and a conceptual scheme which attempts to draw more careful distinctions between social classes, status groups and elites, and between the economic, the political and other elements in social stratification. The value of these new concepts and of the critical revisions of Marx's theory can be better assessed if we now make use of them in an examination of the changes which have taken place in the class structure of some modern societies.

III

CLASSES IN THE INDUSTRIAL SOCIETIES

Tʜᴇ ᴛᴡᴏ broad types of industrial society which I distinguished earlier—capitalist and Soviet—present a number of similar features in their occupational structure and in the general shape of their social stratification, but they also differ widely in their political regimes and their social doctrines and policies, in the manner in which the upper social strata are constituted, and in the historical changes of social structure which they have undergone. It is desirable, therefore, to begin by examining each type of society separately, before attempting any comparison.

In the mid-nineteenth century England was generally regarded as showing most fully and clearly the typical class structure of the new capitalist society.

Marx chose England as his model for studying the development of capitalism and the formation of the principal modern classes—*bourgeoisie* and proletariat —although he associated with this a model of class conflict and revolution which he derived mainly from the experiences of France. Disraeli, who was not a revolutionary, documented in *Sybil* and in other writings the formation of "two nations" within English society, warned against the dangers springing from this rift between the manufacturers and the industrial workers, and at the same time sought to turn it to advantage by enlisting the support of working men for the Tory party against the Liberals. The English class system had, however, some peculiar features which arose, according to R. H. Tawney, from "the blend of a crude plutocratic reality with the sentimental aroma of an aristocratic legend."[1] It was this set of circumstances —still to be exhaustively studied and explained by historians—which created in England the "gentleman ideal" and the public schools as agencies for consolidating and transmitting it. It produced also the snobbery of the middle classes, the "religion of inequality" as Matthew Arnold called it, which maintained fine but strict social distinctions at which foreign observers marvelled.

What changes has this system undergone in the past century? The plutocratic reality, it may be said, has been altered by changes in the distribution of property and income, and above all by the general improvement

[1] R. H. Tawney, *Equality* (4th ed.; London, 1952), p. 57.

in the levels of living. At the end of the nineteenth century severe poverty was still widespread. Charles Booth's survey of London,[2] carried out between 1887 and 1891, showed that at that time more than 30 per cent of the inhabitants were living in poverty; and similar conclusions emerged from Rowntree's study of social conditions in York,[3] begun in 1899. At the other end of the social hierarchy, in the years 1911–13, a privileged 1 per cent of the population owned 68 per cent of all private property and received 29 per cent of the total national income.

The attack upon economic inequality is of very recent date. An estate duty was first imposed towards the end of the nineteenth century, and only in 1949 did it reach the substantial rate of 80 per cent on estates above £1 million. Even so, these rates of taxation reduce large fortunes (and the resulting unearned incomes) very slowly, if at all, since they are counteracted by various forms of tax avoidance, and by capital gains in periods of economic expansion, which can quickly restore fortunes diminished by taxation as well as creating new ones. In 1946–7, 1 per cent of the population still owned 50 per cent of all private property, and it is unlikely that the proportion has changed very much since then. The traditional wealthy class has obviously retained most of its wealth. As Anthony Sampson has observed, "the aristocracy are, in general, much

[2] Charles Booth, *Life and Labour of the People in London* (1902).
[3] B. Seebohm Rowntree, *Poverty; A Study of Town Life* (1901).

richer than they seem. With democracy has come discretion. Their London palaces and outward show have disappeared, but the countryside is still full of millionaire peers: many of them, with the boom in property, are richer now than they have ever been."[4] The observation is probably just as true of wealthy financial or manufacturing families.

The distribution of income is affected by several factors other than the distribution of wealth—by the state of employment, collective bargaining, general social policy, and taxation. During the present century taxes upon income have been used increasingly in attempts to bring about a redistribution between rich and poor; and whereas in 1913 those with earned incomes of £10,000 a year or above paid only about 8 per cent of their income in direct taxation, in 1948 those in the same category paid 75 per cent or more in direct taxation. R. H. Tawney, in the epilogue to the 1952 edition of his *Equality*, noted that the number of incomes exceeding £6,000 a year after payment of tax had declined to a very small figure, and that whereas in 1938 the average retained income of those in the highest category (£10,000 a year and above) was twenty-eight times as great as the income of those in the lowest category (£250–£499 a year), in 1948 it was only thirteen times as great.

However, the tax returns do not provide anything like a complete picture of the distribution of income, and R. M. Titmuss, in the most thorough study of the

4 Anthony Sampson, *Anatomy of Britain* (New York, 1962), pp. 4–5.

question which has yet been made,[5] points to the influence of life assurances, superannuation, tax-free payments on retirement, education covenants, discretionary trusts, expense accounts and capital gains, in conserving or increasing the wealth and income of the upper class. With the present inadequate data it is impossible to arrive at a precise statement of the changes in income distribution which have occurred during the twentieth century. Most students of the problem, however, have concluded that from 1900 to 1939 there was little or no redistribution of income in favour of wage-earners, and that at the end of the period some 10 per cent of the population received almost half the national income while the other 90 per cent of the population received the other half; that between 1939 and 1949 redistribution may have transferred some 10 per cent of the national income from property-owners to wage-earners; but that since 1949 there has again been growing inequality. These calculations are based largely upon the income tax returns, and so they do not take account of the other sources of real income mentioned above, which benefit mainly the rich.

Both Rowntree and Booth concluded from their investigations that two of the most important causes of poverty were the lack of regular employment and the expenses of protracted ill-health. The improvement in the conditions of life for the working class in postwar Britain obviously owes much to the maintenance of full employment and to the development of the health

[5] R. M. Titmuss, *Income Distribution and Social Change* (Toronto, 1962).

services.[6] Full employment, besides raising the level
of income of the working class and providing a degree
of that economic security which the upper class has
always taken for granted, has almost entirely eliminated the class of domestic servants; and this is one of
the greatest gains which the working class has made
in the twentieth century, in escaping from one particularly onerous form of subjection to another class.[7]

It may be argued, too, that the social services as a
whole have a much greater effect in diminishing class
differences than would appear from their economic consequences alone. As R. H. Tawney wrote:

There are certain gross and crushing disabilities—conditions of
life injurious to health, inferior education, economic insecurity
. . . which place the classes experiencing them at a permanent
disadvantage with those not similarly afflicted. There are certain
services by which these crucial disabilities have been greatly
mitigated, and, given time and will, can be altogether removed.
. . . The contribution to equality made by these dynamic agencies is obviously out of all proportion greater than that which
would result from an annual present to every individual among
the forty odd millions concerned of a sum equivalent to his
quota of the total cost.[8]

The social services do not only help to create an equality
in the vital conditions of life for all citizens; so far as
they are used by everyone the standard of the service

[6] Rowntreee emphasizes the importance of these factors in his third
social survey of York. See B. Seebohm Rowntree and G. R. Lavers,
Poverty and the Welfare State (New York, 1951).

[7] Marx observed in *Capital,* Vol. I, that the vast increase in the
numbers of domestic servants, of whom there were well over a million in 1861, showed clearly the growing divergence between the
classes; with wealth and luxury concentrated at one extreme, poverty
and servitude at the other.

[8] R. H. Tawney, *Equality*, p. 248.

tends to rise. It may well be true, as some have argued, that the middle classes have benefited at least as much as the working class from the expansion of the social services, but one important consequence has been that, for example, the standards of free medical care have been vastly improved as compared with the time when such care was provided only for the poor and needy. In the field of education a similar progress is evident since the Education Act of 1944, although here class differences have proved more tenacious and difficult to overcome, while the existence of a large private sector of education has meant that there has been less vigour in the drive to improve the standard of the public service.

We must conclude that the general advance in the material conditions of the British working class, in recent decades, has been due overwhelmingly to the rapid growth of national income, which has also made possible the expansion of the social services, and not to any radical redistribution of wealth or income between classes. Moreover, even in this more affluent society a great deal of poverty remains. Its significance for the relations between classes is, however, very different from that which it had in the nineteenth century. Then, poverty was the lot of a whole class, and there was no expectation that it could be quickly alleviated within the limits of the capitalist economic system. It separated one class in society distinctly from others, and at the same time engendered a movement of revolt. In present-day Britain, as in other advanced industrial countries,

[42]

poverty has ceased to be of this kind; it is now less extensive, and is confined to particular groups in the population—mainly old people and workers in certain occupations or regions which have been left behind as a result of technological progress—which are too isolated or heterogeneous to form the basis of a radical social movement. These impoverished groups stand in marked contrast with the majority of the working class, which enjoys a high level of living in relation both to past societies and to some middle-class groups in present-day society.

The thesis of *embourgeoisement*, which was briefly examined in the previous chapter, relies in the main for its factual basis upon this improvement in levels of living and the changes in the relative economic position of manual workers and some sections of white-collar workers, but it also brings in the effects of social mobility in modifying the class system. Since the war, sociologists have studied social mobility much more intensively than they have studied the changes within classes themselves, and they have attributed much importance to it as a solvent of class divisions. The findings of recent studies[9] may be summarized in the following way. Social mobility has generally increased with the economic development of the industrial societies, but the increase

[9] See especially, D. V. Glass (ed.), *Social Mobility in Britain* (New York, 1955). This comprehensive study, based mainly upon a national sample survey, has provided a model for a number of later investigations in other countries. For comparative studies which bring together much recent research see S. M. Lipset and R. Bendix, *Social Mobility in Industrial Society* (Berkeley, 1959), and S. M. Miller, "Comparative Social Mobility," *Current Sociology*, IX (1), 1960.

has been due very largely to changes in the occupational structure; that is, to the expansion of white-collar and professional occupations and the contraction of manual occupations. For this reason, S. M. Miller has suggested that sociologists ought to give more attention to "downward mobility," which involves a real exchange of occupational and social position between classes and may well be "a better indicator of fluidity in a society than is upward mobility."[10]

A second important feature is that most social mobility takes place between social levels which are close together; for example, between the upper levels of the working class and the lower levels of the middle class. Movement from the working class into the upper class is very limited in any society, and notably so in Britain.[11] This characteristic can be shown more clearly by studies of recruitment to particular elite occupations such as the higher civil service, business management and the older professions. In Britain, a study of the directors of large public companies reveals that more than half of them began their careers with the advantage of having business connections in the family, while another 40 per cent came from families of landowners, professional men and others of similar social position.[12] A study of higher civil servants in the administrative class shows that 30 per cent came from

[10] S. M. Miller, op. cit., p. 59.
[11] Ibid., p. 40.
[12] G. H. Copeman, *Leaders of British Industry; A Study of the Careers of More Than a Thousand Public Company Directors* (London, 1955).

families of the upper and upper middle classes, and another 40 per cent from the intermediate levels of the middle class, while only 3 per cent were recruited from families of semiskilled and unskilled manual workers.[13] Nevertheless, the same study indicates that the area of recruitment of high civil servants has been extended somewhat during the past thirty years, and the same may well be true in the case of other professions.

The main influence here has been the extension of educational opportunities; and the view that social mobility has increased substantially in postwar Britain derives very largely from the belief that educational reforms have provided vast new opportunities for upward movement. It is certainly true that before the war social mobility was restricted especially by financial and other obstacles in the way of access to secondary and higher education.[14] The Education Act of 1944 established for the first time a national system of secondary education and greatly increased the opportunities for working-class children to obtain a grammar school education.[15] Also in the postwar period the access of working-class children to university has been made somewhat easier by the increase of student num-

[13] R. K. Kelsall, *Higher Civil Servants in Britain* (New York, 1955).

[14] See data presented in L. Hogben (ed.), *Political Arithmetic* (New York, 1938).

[15] D. V. Glass notes, in his introduction to *Social Mobility in Britain,* that in one region, S. W. Hertfordshire, between the 1930s and 1951, "the proportion of children of manual workers in the total entry to grammar schools rose from about 15 per cent to 43 per cent." See also the material given in J. E. Floud, A. H. Halsey and F. M. Martin, *Social Class and Educational Opportunity* (London, 1957).

bers and the more lavish provision of maintenance grants. Nevertheless, Britain is still very far from having equality of opportunity in education. The existence of a private sector of school education, misleadingly called the "public schools," maintains the educational and occupational advantages of upper-class families, while in the state system of education, although the opportunities for working-class children have increased, it is probable that middle-class families have actually made greater use of the new opportunities for grammar school and university education.[16] Even if we add to the social mobility which takes place through the educational system, that which may be assumed to occur as a result of the growth of new middle-class occupations—for example, in the entertainments industry—where educational qualifications are less important, it can still not be said that the movement of individuals in the social hierarchy is very considerable or is increasing rapidly. The vast majority of people still remain in their class of origin.

It may be questioned, too, whether even a much higher rate of social mobility, involving an interchange between classes in which downward mobility was roughly equal to upward mobility, would have much effect upon the class system, in the sense of reducing the barriers or the antagonism between classes. On the contrary, in such a situation of high mobility, the work-

[16] Appendix Two (B) to the *Report on Higher Education* (Cmnd. 2154) observes that the proportion of university students coming from working-class families remained almost unchanged (at about 25 per cent) between 1928–47 and 1961.

ing class would come to comprise those who had failed to rise in the social hierarchy in spite of the opportunities available to them, and those who had descended, through personal failure, from higher social levels; and such a class, made up of particularly embittered and frustrated individuals, might be expected to be very sharply distinguished from, and in conflict with, the rest of society. There are apparent, indeed, in Britain and in other industrial societies, some elements of such a condition among the younger generations in the population.

The most important aspect of social mobility is perhaps the impression which it makes upon the public consciousness. According to the type and degree of social mobility a society may appear to its members to be "open" and fluid, presenting manifold opportunities to talent and energy, or it may appear to be rigid and "closed." In Britain, all manner of ancient institutions and modes of behaviour—the aristocracy, the public schools, Oxbridge, differences of speech and accent, the relationships of the "old boy" network—frustrate mobility and buttress the public conception of a rigidly hierarchical society. Any increase in social mobility, even in the past two decades, has been too modest, gradual and discreet to create a new outlook. The boundaries of class may have become more blurred, chiefly at the lower levels of the social hierarchy and there may have been some expansion of opportunities, especially in the sphere of consumption, for large sections of the population. But there is no general sense of greater "classlessness," nor of great opportunities for the individual to choose and create his way of life regardless of inherited wealth or social position.

It was in the general acceptance of an egalitarian ideology, which still persists in some degree, that the USA differed most remarkably from the European societies in the nineteenth century. In America, there was no established system of feudal ranks, no historical memory of an aristocratic order of society, which could provide a model for a new social hierarchy. The American war of independence indeed was an important influence upon the European revolutions against the *ancien régime*. In the USA, in contrast with the European countries, the ownership of property was quite widely diffused in the early part of the nineteenth century, and some 80 per cent of the working population (excluding the Negro slaves) owned the means of production with which they worked. America was, predominantly, a society of small farmers, small traders and small businessmen; the closest approach there has been to a "property-owning democracy." Of course, disparities of wealth existed, but they were not so extreme as in Europe, and they did not give rise, except in some of the southern states, to disparities of social rank comparable with those in the still aristocratic and oligarchical European societies. De Tocqueville saw in the USA the prime example of a tendency towards equality in modern societies; a society in which, as he wrote: "Great wealth tends to disappear, the number of small fortunes to increase."

The sense of belonging to a society of equals was enhanced by the possibility of easy movement in the still rudimentary hierarchy of wealth. America was the "land of opportunity," a vast, unexplored and unexploited country in which it was always possible, or seemed possible, to escape from economic want or subjection by moving to a new place, acquiring land or some other property, and adding to it by personal effort and talent.

A century and a half of economic change has destroyed most of the foundations upon which the egalitarian ideology rested. The society made up of small property-owners and independent producers began to be undermined soon after the Civil War. The 1880s and 1890s, a period in which industry grew rapidly and modern communications were vastly expanded, saw the "closing of the frontier," the emergence of the first industrial and financial trusts, and a considerable growth of inequalities of wealth. Class divisions began to appear more clearly, and to resemble more closely those in the European societies, and they were more openly asserted. The conscious emergence of an upper class was signalled by the establishment of the *Social Register* (the guide to the new American "aristocracy"), and by the foundation of exclusive boarding schools and country clubs; and wealth and social position came increasingly to be transmitted through family connections. At the same time the working class became more strongly organized in trade unions and political associations, and from the 1890s to the 1930s there were numerous attempts, though without any lasting success, to bring these associations together in a broad socialist movement.

The changes in the economic system can be documented clearly from the statistics of occupations. Early in the nineteenth century 80 per cent of the employed white population were independent (self-employed) producers; by 1870 only 41 per cent were self-employed, and by 1940 only 18 per cent. In the words of C. Wright Mills:

Over the last hundred years, the United States has been transformed from a nation of small capitalists into a nation of hired employees; but the ideology suitable for the nation of small capitalists persists, as if that small-propertied world were still a going concern.[17]

There are several reasons for the persistence of this inapt ideology, apart from the inertia which characterizes social doctrines in general. One is that the concentration of property ownership was not accompanied by any sudden expansion of the working class, or by any decline in the level of living. The industrial workers formed 28 per cent of the population in 1870, and 31 per cent in 1940; and wage-earners as a whole made up 53 per cent of the population in 1870, and 57 per cent in 1940. During the same period, however, the proportion of salaried employees in the population increased very rapidly, from 7 per cent to 25 per cent; and this expansion of the new white-collar middle classes made possible a new kind of social mobility, in place of that which had been achieved earlier by the settlement of fresh lands.

[17] C. Wright Mills, *White Collar: The American Middle Classes* (New York, 1951), p. 34.

Again, the concentration of wealth and income in a few hands seems never to have proceeded so far in America as in many European countries; and the gilded age of spectacular fortunes in the midst of widespread poverty lasted for a relatively short time. As in other industrial countries, there has been a persistent effort to redistribute wealth and income in the USA through progressive taxation, estate duties, and taxes on capital gains. Since the war, the continued economic expansion, rising levels of living, and the steady growth of the middle classes have had their effect upon the class structure in the same way as in other countries, but in a more conspicuous fashion. And whilst in Britain, for example, such changes have so far produced only modifications and questionings of a class system which is still extremely solid and which profoundly affects political life, in America they have brought instead confirmation of an inherited ideology of "classlessness" and have practically extinguished the tentative class consciousness which found expression in the politics of the 1930s.

This divergence is not to be explained by a higher rate of social mobility in the USA in recent times, nor by a more rapid progress in the redistribution of wealth and income. Several studies have indicated that the USA does not have a rate of mobility significantly higher than that of some other industrial societies, in which class consciousness is nevertheless much more intense.[18] This is the case, at least, when the broad

[18] See especially, S. M. Lipset and R. Bendix, *Social Mobility in Industrial Society*.

movement from manual to non-manual occupations is considered. The long-range movement from the manual strata into the elites does seem to be greater in the USA than in most other countries;[19] but even so, it has not been very considerable at any time during the present century. William Miller has shown that even in the first decade of the century successful businessmen had not generally risen from the lower strata of society, but had come for the most part from old established families in the business and professional strata.[20] Similarly, a very thorough study of social classes in Philadelphia has revealed that the leading positions in the economic system are occupied predominantly by individuals from the established upper-class families.[21]

The idea that a steady reduction of income inequalities has been proceeding during the present century is strongly contested, just as a similar view is contested in Britain. In the case of the USA the contention rests largely upon the statistical studies of national income by Simon Kuznets;[22] but as Gabriel Kolko has recently pointed out,[23] the relevant part of these studies deals only with the wealthiest 5 per cent of the population, and does not examine the changes which have taken

[19] S. M. Miller, op. cit., p. 58.

[20] "American Historians and the Business Elite," in William Miller (ed.), *Men in Business* (new ed.; New York, 1962).

[21] E. Digby Baltzell, *An American Business Aristocracy* (new ed.; New York, 1962).

[22] See especially his *Shares of Upper Income Groups in Income and Savings* (Princeton, 1952).

[23] Gabriel Kolko, *Wealth and Power in America* (rev. ed.; New York, 1964).

place in the incomes of other groups in the population.
Kolko's own calculations, based upon studies of personal incomes before taxation by the National Industrial
Conference Board (for 1910–37) and by the Survey
Research Center (for 1941–59) indicate that between
1910 and 1959 the share in national income of the top
income-tenth declined only slightly (and has fluctuated
around 30 per cent in the past decade), while the shares
of the second and third income-tenths actually increased and the shares of the two poorest income-tenths
declined sharply (from 8.3 per cent of national income
to only 4 per cent). Kolko also observes, as Titmuss
has done in his study of the same question in Britain,
that calculations based upon declarations of pretax income necessarily leave out of account various forms of
real income which benefit mainly the upper class and
thus increase inequality.

It may be argued, then, that it is the traditional conception of American society as highly mobile rather
than any exceptional degree of mobility at the present
time, and the general increase in prosperity (though
with a good deal of partially concealed poverty)[24]
rather than any strong movement towards greater economic equality, which play the main part in weakening class consciousness. But there have also been other

[24] See, on the extent of poverty, Gunnar Myrdal, *Challenge to Affluence* (New York, 1963), Chapter 4, and Michael Harrington, *The
Other America* (New York, 1962). The latter book makes plain that
poverty is widespread, but (as in Britain) it is concentrated in particular sections of the population—here among the old, ethnic minorities, and workers in such regions as the Appalachians—and so often
tends to go unrecognized.

factors at work, especially in inhibiting the development of a working class movement in which the ideas of class interest, and of socialism as an alternative form of society, would have a major influence. Among these factors, the situation of the Negroes and the successive waves of immigration are particularly important. The Negroes have formed a distinctive American proletariat, with the lowest incomes, the most menial and subservient tasks, and the lowest social prestige (in part because of their slave origins) of any group in American society. The existence of this large, relatively homogeneous, easily identifiable, and exploited group has meant that every white American, even the lowest-paid labourer, possesses a certain social prestige which raises him, at least in his own view, above the level of a proletarian. Immigration has worked in the same way to raise the social position of the ordinary American worker, since many groups of immigrants (the latest being the Puerto Ricans) entered the lowest levels of the occupational hierarchy, and made it possible for those already established to advance themselves. But neither the Negroes, nor any immigrant group, have formed a proletariat in the sense that they have challenged the established order of society. And so, although the present vigorous struggle of the Negroes to gain full economic, civil and political rights may be likened to early class conflicts in Europe so far as these were concerned with the right to vote, with labour legislation and with social reform, it differs entirely from these conflicts in so far as it aims exclusively at winning acceptance in the existing society and accepts the predominant values of that society. The success of the struggles waged by Negroes and other ethnic minorities, however, would diminish the importance of ethnic divisions in American society, and one result might be the appearance of more sharply differentiated social classes and a greater awareness of class interests.

Against this development, however, there are working the same influences which we have seen in Britain: a more or less continuous rise in levels of living; a greater differentiation of the occupational structure, and so a more complex type of social stratification; a relative decline of manual occupations; and an expansion of educational opportunities which has already gone much farther in America than in other countries. These influences are at work in all the Western capitalist societies; in France, Germany and Italy, where, in the past, class divisions have been deeper and class conflicts more violent than in Britain, and equally in the Scandinavian countries, in which social welfare and equality of opportunity have advanced farther than elsewhere. The consequences are to be seen in a relative appeasement of bitter conflicts over the structure of society as a whole, and in a displacement of political interest towards new problems of technological advance, economic growth and modernization. The two cultures have replaced the two nations as a subject of political debate, at least for many Western intellectuals. Whether the changes in social conditions and attitudes have actually brought about, or will bring about, a consolidation of the present social structure in the Western countries, and what other political consequences they are likely to have, are questions which I shall consider later on.

Our immediate concern is to examine the evolution of classes in the Soviet type of industrial society. According to Marx's view modern capitalism would be "the last antagonistic form of the process of production." As he wrote in *The Poverty of Philosophy:*

The condition for the emancipation of the working class is the abolition of all classes. . . . The working class, in the course of its development, will substitute for the old civil society an association which will exclude classes and their antagonism.

The USSR, although the revolution which created it did not take place in a highly industrialized country, does nevertheless claim to be a society of the kind which Marx predicted would follow the destruction of capitalism. It claims, that is, to be a classless society, at least in the sense that there is no hierarchy of classes and no domination by one class over others. This claim is based mainly upon the fact that the private ownership of the means of production has been abolished. Social theorists in the USSR have rarely attempted to analyse the social and political foundations of a classless society, and for long periods, especially after 1930, they were at some pains to make a sharp distinction between "classlessness" and "egalitarianism." The latter was denounced as a "petty bourgeois deviation," and the Soviet Encyclopaedia of Stalin's time asserted that "socialism and egalitarianism have nothing in common."[25]

[25] An English Socialist, on the other hand, has written: "Where there is no egalitarianism there is no Socialism." Roy Jenkins, "Equality" in *New Fabian Essays* (New York, 1952).

This ideological offensive against egalitarianism coincided broadly with the change in policy of the Soviet rulers in the early 1930s, which involved increasing wage and salary differentials, and in particular offering substantial financial incentives to highly skilled workers, scientists and technicians, industrial managers and intellectuals. These policies were continued during and after the war, and as a result the range of incomes in the USSR came to be almost as great as that in the capitalist countries. It is estimated that in 1953 industrial incomes ranged between 3,500–5,000 roubles a year for an unskilled worker, and 80,000–120,000 roubles for an important factory manager. The top incomes were, therefore, some 25–30 times as great as those at the bottom, which is perhaps somewhat less than the difference in Britain or the USA between the income of an unskilled worker and that of a managing director. But when the effects of taxation are considered, the income range in the USSR may have been greater, for the Soviet income tax is not steeply progressive, and taxation as a whole is regressive, since the greater part of the budget income is derived from a turnover tax on food and textile goods of mass consumption. These inequalities of income have been enhanced by other factors: by the abolition of the progressive inheritance tax in 1943, and by the privileges accorded to the higher social strata in education and housing, in the use of special shops, the acquisition of cars and other scarce goods, and the award of prizes, grants and annuities.

The policy of increasing income differentiation could

be explained by the demands of rapid industrialization in the 1930s, and later by the needs of war and post-war reconstruction. This is not, I think, the whole explanation; but in so far as it contains some truth, we might infer that with the completion of the stage of rapid industrialization (which Rostow has called the "drive to maturity") in the USSR, there would be a slackening, or even a reversal, of the trend towards greater inequality. A recent study[26] suggests that this is in fact happening. The author observes that since 1956 a number of policy statements have emphasized the raising of minimum wages, and he quotes the programme of the 22nd Congress of the CPSU to the effect that in the next twenty years "the disparity between high and comparatively low incomes must be steadily reduced."[27] He goes on to calculate, from Soviet statistics, which have become more abundant in recent years, that wage differentials have declined considerably since 1956; for example, whereas the average earnings of engineering technical personnel exceeded those of manual workers by two and a half times in the early 1930s, they were only 50 per cent higher in 1960. He concludes: "The period since 1956 has been marked by a narrowing of skill differentials in wage rates, substantial increases in minimum wages, and the declining importance of the piece-rate system."[28]

Even at the time when the inegalitarian features of

[26] Murray Yanowitch, "The Soviet Income Revolution," *Slavic Review*, XXIII (4), December, 1963.

[27] Ibid., p. 684.

[28] Ibid., p. 692.

Soviet society were so blatant, it was often argued that they did not signify the growth of a new class system. A sympathetic French observer of Soviet society put the argument as follows: "Some people might be tempted to conclude on the basis of this profound wage differentiation that Soviet society has not, in reality, abolished classes. . . . It seems to me that classes as they exist in Western countries have actually no true equivalent in the USSR. The prejudices based on wealth, rigid barriers, the organized opposition of one class to its enlargement from below—these no longer exist or are in process of disappearing for ever in the Soviet Union. Widespread education, the encouragement profusely given by the authorities to the social advance of those elements which have been less well placed to start with—all this points towards a final result that may legitimately be termed a 'classless society.' . . . That is why, if anyone may argue about the presence or absence of classes in the USSR, one must in any case recognize that the upper classes are abundantly open to members of the lower classes, and that the privileged levels have nothing of crystallization, rigidity, or especially heredity about them."[29]

The high rate of social mobility and the absence of important barriers against mobility have often been adduced in this way as evidence for the gradual disappearance of social classes in the USSR. But the argument is open to several objections. In the first place,

[29] Michel Gordey, *Visa to Moscow* (English trans.; New York, 1952).

[59]

there has been no comprehensive study of social mobility in the USSR which would permit such definite assertions about its rate, either in absolute terms or in comparison with other societies.[30] Social mobility may have been considerable in the past half century, but it can be explained by the rapid industrialization of the country and by losses in war (that is, by the same factors as in some Western countries) rather than by any distinctive features of the social structure. Industrial development created an array of new positions in the higher levels of the social hierarchy, and while the employed population doubled between 1926 and 1937, the intelligentsia (officials, professional and scientific workers, managers and clerical workers) increased nearly four times. The increase in certain occupations was even more spectacular; the numbers of engineers and architects increased nearly eight times, and the numbers of scientific workers nearly six times.[31]

The process of expansion of white-collar occupations is still continuing, but in the USSR as in other industrial countries, the rate of expansion is likely to slow down as industrial maturity is reached (if we exclude, for

[30] One of the very few sources of data is the Harvard study of Soviet émigrés; see Alex Inkeles and R. A. Bauer, *The Soviet Citizen: Daily Life in a Totalitarian Society* (Cambridge, Mass., 1959). This is obviously not a study of a representative sample, but such as it is it indicates that the amount of movement from manual into nonmanual occupations as a whole is not exceptionally high in the USSR when compared with some Western societies, but that movement from the manual strata into the elites is particularly high. (For these comparisons see S. M. Miller, op. cit.)

[31] See S. M. Schwartz, *Labor in the Soviet Union* (New York, 1952).

the present, the possible effects of automation), and the degree of mobility will come to depend more directly upon social policies designed to promote the interchange of individuals between the various social strata. In the later years of Stalin's regime, there were some indications that social mobility was being restricted, while the social privileges of the upper strata were more strongly emphasized. One step in this direction was the introduction, in 1940, of fees in higher education and in the last three years of secondary education. This increased the existing bias in favour of the upper strata in the selection of university students, and thus of the next generation of the intelligentsia. The reservation of high positions for those in the upper strata was aided by the new inheritance laws and by the strengthening of family ties.[32]

Nevertheless, the upper levels of Soviet society probably remained fairly open and accessible to talented individuals from the lower strata, and in recent years there have been attempts to deal with those influences which restrict mobility, for example in the sphere of education. Such efforts have been helped by the general movement to curb privilege and to bring about a greater equality of economic condition. Even at the time when income inequalities were increasing, there were other factors which made for social equality over a large part of Soviet society. There was, and is, no real "leisure class" in the USSR; and the fact that so-

[32] See Alex Inkeles, "Social Stratification and Mobility in the Soviet Union," *American Sociological Review*, August, 1950.

cial status depends mainly upon occupation—that is, upon a definite contribution to the well-being of society (however arbitrarily the relative value of the contributions may be determined in some cases)—limits the social effects of economic differences. It seems clear from the experience of Western countries that the social distinctions based upon property ownership and inheritance are more strongly felt, and are more divisive in their effects, than those which arise from differences in earned income. Again, the divisions created in the USSR by income differences were moderated by the fact that some skilled manual workers were also highly paid, while others could improve their position through activity in the party organizations; and still more by the absence of such profound social and cultural differences between manual and non-manual workers as exist in most of the Western countries.[33]

Yet in the opinion of many sociologists the facts we have been considering do not bear directly upon the most significant aspect of the class structure in Soviet society. However "classless" social relationships may be at some levels of society, is there not, in the Soviet

[33] The separation between manual workers and non-manual workers in the Western countries in leisure-time activities is well established by sociological research. On France, see especially P. H. Chombart de Lauwe, *Paris et L'Agglomération Parisienne* (Paris, 1952); on England, T. B. Bottomore, "Social Stratification in Voluntary Organizations" in D. V. Glass (ed.), *Social Mobility in Britain*. Numerous studies, from R. A. and H. M. Lynd's *Middletown* (New York, 1929) to recent investigations of voluntary associations, point to the same phenomenon in the USA. This separation is beginning to break down, perhaps, with rising levels of living, but there is little evidence as yet to show any radical change.

type of society, a governing elite which resembles closely the ruling classes of other societies, except that its power is more concentrated and less subject to restraint? Milovan Djilas, in *The New Class*, has argued that the Communist party officials in these societies have come to constitute a new ruling class which, in his words, is "made up of those who have special privileges and economic preference because of the administrative monopoly they hold."[34] Similarly, Stanislaw Ossowski, in the work quoted earlier, emphasizes the extent to which in the modern world, and especially in the Soviet countries, changes in the class structure are brought about by the decisions of political authorities; or as he says later, by compulsion or force.[35] Thus classes no longer arise spontaneously from the economic activities of individuals; instead a political elite imposes upon society the type of stratification to be found in a bureaucratic hierarchy.

The most comprehensive expression of this view has been given by Raymond Aron in two articles published in 1950,[36] and more recently in his book *La Lutte de classes*.[37] Aron asserts that the members of the ruling group in Soviet society have

infinitely more power than the political rulers in a democratic society, because both political and economic power are con-

[34] Op. cit., p. 39.

[35] S. Ossowski, *Class Structure in the Social Consciousness* (London, 1963), pp. 184, 186.

[36] Raymond Aron, "Social Structure and the Ruling Class," *British Journal of Sociology*, I (1), March, 1950, and I (2), June, 1950.

[37] Raymond Aron, *La Lutte de classes* (Paris, 1964). See especially Chapters 9 and 10.

centrated in their hands. . . . Politicians, trade-union leaders, public officials, generals and managers all belong to one party and are part of an authoritarian organization. The unified elite has absolute and unbounded power.[38]

Another element in its power is the ideological monopoly which it enjoys through its control of the exposition and interpretation of an official creed—Marxism—which shapes the thoughts and opinions of the people and provides justifications for the actions of the ruling group. Aron contrasts this unified Soviet elite with the divided elite, or plurality of elites, in the democratic capitalist countries, and he seeks to explain the difference by the presence or absence of classes and other autonomous interest groups in the society.

These observers agree in discovering a profound division in Soviet society between the ruling elite and the rest of the population. Are they right in supposing that this signifies the formation of a new class system? Or is it only a temporary feature in a movement towards a genuinely classless society? Defenders of the Soviet regime have portrayed the Stalinist period—during which the privileges of the upper stratum, political dictatorship, and rule by violence attained an extreme point—as an historical aberration, resulting from what is now termed the "cult of personality." But this is no explanation. The cult of personality has itself to be explained, and this is all the more necessary and urgent since its appearance contradicts all the expectations which Marxists had about the nature of a classless

[38] Article cit., *British Journal of Sociology*, I (2), p. 131.

society. An explanation might be attempted by stating the social conditions which are favourable to the rise of charismatic leaders, along the lines which Max Weber first suggested. In the particular instance of the USSR we could point to such features as the sudden break with the past in the revolution, and the stresses, together with the need for authority and discipline, engendered by the rapid industrialization of an economically backward country. Or else, we may look for more general conditions which favour a unified elite, as Aron does when he argues that a "classless society" (in the restricted sense of a society in which all economic enterprises are publicly owned and managed) necessarily produces a great concentration of power in the hands of the political and industrial leaders; and as Ossowski does when he suggests that political power has now become so important in all the industrial countries, but especially in the Soviet countries, that the political elite is able to form and change the system of stratification rather than being itself a product of that system.

These ideas are at variance with Marx's conception of the relation between property ownership, social classes and political power; and also with his account of how the class system in modern societies would develop. The great extension of the activities of government, in economic development and in the provision of social services; the growth of highly organized and powerful political parties; the influence which can be exerted through the modern media of communication: these have all worked to establish a major division in society between the governing elite—which may include political and military leaders, high officials, and the directors of important economic enterprises—and the mass of the population, to some extent independently of social classes based upon property ownership, or of other forms of stratification. In the USSR, where this division is most firmly established—because the political rulers belong to a party, revolutionary in origin, which has an exceptionally rigorous organization, and which is further bound together by an all-embracing ideology—it is also most profoundly obscured, because the doctrine to which the ruling elite adheres excludes either recognition or investigation of such a phenomenon.

At least, this has been the case until recently. Now at last some fresh life appears to be stirring in the long insensible body of orthodox Marxism; and not only are Marx's ideas and theories being re-examined in a more critical spirit, but the social structure of the Soviet countries is beginning to be studied in a more realistic and objective manner. As a result, the problems of the centralization of power are now more open to rational discussion; and the attempts to combine public ownership and central planning with the creation of relatively independent local centres of decision, such as are being made in Yugoslavia through the institutions of workers' self-management, are no longer rejected out of hand as sinister deviations from orthodoxy. The Yugoslav experience, in fact, seems to many socialists (Marxist and other) to hold out the promise of an eventual classless society in which there would be neither political dictatorship nor total intellectual conformity. At the same time it illustrates very strikingly the newly tolerated diversity of institutions and doctrines within the Soviet group of countries.

The capitalist societies, as we have seen already, are also diverse in their class structure, and any comparison between the Soviet and the capitalist forms of industrial society must recognize that there is a considerable range of variation within each type of society —for example, in the nature and extent of social mobility, in the magnitude of economic inequalities, in the situation of the working class and in the degree of unification of the elite—which makes for a continuum of differences rather than an abrupt break between the two types. This fact, which is unpalatable to the more extreme ideologists on both sides, is given further emphasis by the common features in Soviet and capitalist societies which result mainly from three important influences upon all modern societies: the rapid progress of industrialization, the growing size of organizations, especially in the economic sphere, and the increasing part played by governments in the deliberate shaping of economic and social life.

Industrialization has sometimes been regarded by sociologists as a process which tends naturally to bring about a greater equality of conditions in society. This view is supported by various arguments. The development of industry breaks down any rigid and exclusive differences of rank, by creating unprecedented opportunities for social mobility, by extending and improving education to meet the new scientific and technological needs, and by raising enormously the general level of living, thus reducing the harshness of the contrast between the conditions of the upper and lower strata of society. Furthermore, modern industry, by increasing the size of societies, as well as the amount of mobility, creates circumstances which are especially favourable to the diffusion of egalitarian ideas, as Bouglé attempted to show in a work, now much neglected, on *Les Idées égalitaires;*[39] and at the same time it brings into being a large and articulate social group —the industrial workers—capable of initiating a political movement which gives a great impetus to the spread of egalitarian and democratic ideas.

This relationship between industrialization and social stratification can be seen very well in the present-day developing countries. In many of them there are, or have been until recently, extremes of wealth and poverty much greater than those in the industrial countries; and the traditional upper classes have constituted a formidable obstacle to economic development, by their general resistance to change and mobility, and by their propensity to use the large share of the national income which they receive for conspicuous consumption rather than productive investment. Where industrialization gets under way successfully it is very often at the expense of upper-class wealth and privileges, through confiscation or high taxation, and the opening of elite occupations to talented individuals from the lower social

[39] C. Bouglé, *Les Idées égalitaires: Étude sociologique* (Paris, 1925).

strata. Conversely, where, as in India, an extraordinarily intricate and inflexible traditional form of stratification successfully resists any radical changes, the pace of industrialization may be greatly diminished, and the whole endeavour to promote economic growth be put in jeopardy.

It would be quite wrong, however, to suppose that industrialization leads inexorably to an egalitarian society. The evidence we have already considered shows that in the Western industrial societies there has been little reduction of economic inequality in the past few decades, while in the USSR inequality actually increased between the 1930s and the 1950s, to some extent as part of a policy of incentives to induce more rapid industrialization. Moreover, the other influences at work in modern societies, mentioned earlier, tend to increase social inequality, by accentuating the distinction between elites and masses. The increasing size and the growing rationalization of business enterprises has had this effect, by establishing a small group of top managers, supported by expert advisers, in remote control of the routine and largely unskilled activities of large numbers of workers. Other large organizations, including the modern political parties, also display some of the same features. The increasing scope and powers of the central government are another aspect of this process in which the making of important decisions tends to be more and more concentrated in a few hands, while the powers of independent voluntary associations and of local elected bodies decline.

The principal difference between the Soviet countries and the capitalist democracies is to be found in the character of the elites, and its political consequences, rather than in the other aspects of social stratification. As we have seen, the range of incomes in these societies is broadly similar, and everywhere large differences of income produce distinctions between social groups in their styles of life, their opportunities and their social prestige. In the early 1950s, it appeared that economic inequalities were increasing in the Soviet societies and diminishing (though very slowly) in the capitalist societies. At the present time, both these trends seem to have been reversed, but it is difficult as yet to foresee the consequences of these changes. One fact does mark an important contrast: namely, that in the Soviet societies, economic inequalities do not arise to any significant extent from differences in wealth, whereas the distinctions between property-owners and propertyless workers, between income from property and income from work, run all through the capitalist societies, and largely account for the strong sentiments of class position which are manifest there. This circumstance is connected with the fact that the distinctions between whole social groups are less obvious and less emphasized in the Soviet societies. Income differences produce some separation of groups, but it is probably the case that social intercourse between individuals in different occupations and income levels is a great deal easier than in the capitalist countries. One of the major divisions in Soviet society has probably been that between town and country, between urban workers and peasants. How far the gap has diminished in the USSR in recent years it is difficult to determine in the absence of serious research, but studies in other countries— notably in Yugoslavia and Poland—indicate that it is still considerable; and its full extent is shown by the problems of acculturation which arise when peasants are recruited for industrial work in the course of economic development.

The contrast between the unified ruling elite in the Soviet countries and the divided elite in the capitalist democracies, which has been so much emphasized by sociologists during the past decade, has itself to be interpreted with great care if we are to escape the absurd view that in one of these types of society there is a completely monolithic ruling party, while in the other there is no ruling group at all. The Soviet societies approach more or less closely the ideal type of a unified elite, which suppresses any opposition, whether political or intellectual, from other social forces, as well as any conflict within its own ranks; but it is clear that these societies have experienced in practice very serious conflicts between different interest groups, and that in recent years the opportunities for such interest groups to express criticism and to influence policy have increased.

In the capitalist societies, on the other hand, the evident division of the elite into divergent interest groups at one level does not preclude the existence at another level of important *common* interests and aspirations which tend to produce a uniformity of outlook and action on fundamental issues of social policy. The elites in these societies are recruited very largely from an upper class which has its own distinctive economic and cultural interests, and their provenance is likely to shape to a common pattern the ends and forms of action which they adopt. Even where the association between an upper class and the elite groups is less strong the latter may still, by virtue of the manifold connections which are established between those who wield power in various spheres, come to act generally in concert, despite the conflicts between them on particular occasions. This is the principal argument of C. Wright Mills in *The Power Elite;* but he goes further in suggesting that the development of modern society tends to produce, by the centralization of power and the elimination or weakening of local and voluntary associations, a "mass society," the rudiments of which can be discerned everywhere, and which is gradually taking the place of the older form of industrial society with its division into social classes.[40]

However, it is not so much the homogeneity or heterogeneity of the ruling elite as the possibility of forming and establishing organizations which *oppose* the elite in power, which constitutes the principal difference between the Soviet societies and the capitalist democracies. Old-fashioned Marxists explain this disparity very easily, by observing that there are, in the Soviet

[40] C. Wright Mills, *The Power Elite* (New York, 1956), p. 304. ". . . we have moved a considerable distance along the road to the mass society. At the end of that road there is totalitarianism, as in Nazi Germany or in Communist Russia."

[72]

societies, no exploiting or exploited classes, thus no class antagonisms, and thus no basis for political conflict; whereas in the capitalist democracies, it is precisely the existence of classes having opposed interests which engenders the major political conflicts. The second part of this statement is very generally accepted, though with many qualifications which were indicated in our earlier discussion;[41] but the first part will not bear serious examination. In many of the Soviet societies —and especially in the USSR—there have been profound social conflicts, which have erupted from time to time in large-scale revolts; as for example in the resistance of the Russian peasants to collectivization in the 1930s, and in the uprising of the Hungarian people in 1956. If these conflicts have not given rise to any sustained public opposition to the ruling elite it is only because they have been forcibly repressed. The absence of an organized opposition is no indication at all of a state of society in which harmony and co-operation have replaced conflict when it results in this way from the persistent use of violence by the political rulers. Marx was consistent in arguing, from his premises, that with the abolition of classes the major source of political conflict in society would be eliminated, and that the need for a coercive state would then disappear. In the phrase of Saint-Simon, which Marx adopted, "the government of men is replaced by the administration of things." It is all too evident that this is not what has happened in the Soviet societies. On the contrary

[41] See above, pp. 18–20, 25–27.

the repressive apparatus of the state has grown enormously;[42] and although in the USSR and other East European countries the rule of force has been moderated since the death of Stalin, government is still much more coercive than in the capitalist societies. Of late there has been more outspoken criticism; and in some spheres which do not affect very closely the political regime, a greater freedom of thought and imagination has been permitted. The official doctrines of socialist realism in art, music and literature seem, happily, to be expiring. But there is still neither freedom of movement for the individual, nor any possibility of organized public dissent and opposition on important questions of social policy. In certain respects, as in the introduction of the death penalty for various economic offences, the coercive power of the state has been enhanced,[43] and the existence of serious conflict within the society all the more clearly demonstrated.

Two general conclusions may be drawn from this discussion. The first is that the extent of conflict and of coercive government, in the Soviet societies, indi-

[42] Except in Yugoslavia, which has remained largely outside the sphere of influence of the USSR.

[43] Marx himself consistently opposed the coercive power of the state, and he expressed himself forthrightly on the subject of capital punishment, in a passage which is peculiarly apposite to the present conditions in the Soviet countries: "Now, what a state of society is that which knows of no better instrument for its own defence than the hangman, and which proclaims . . . its own brutality as eternal law? . . . is there not a necessity for deeply reflecting upon an alteration of the system that breeds these crimes, instead of glorifying the hangman who executes a lot of criminals to make room only for the supply of new ones?" "Capital Punishment," *New York Daily Tribune*, February 18, 1853.

cates either that classes and class antagonisms have survived or have been re-created in a new form in these societies; or else that there are other important sources of social conflicts besides those of class interest, and that if, through the influence of a doctrinaire creed such conflicts are denied expression, this can only be accomplished in the last resort by violence. The second conclusion is that if the main source of political and ideological conflicts in the modern capitalist societies has been the opposition between classes, and if such conflicts have helped to establish some of the vital conditions of democracy—the right of dissent and criticism, the right to create associations independently of the state—then it must be considered whether the abolition, or even the decline, of social classes does not open the way for the growth of a mass society, in which the political elite has unbounded power, just as much as for the creation of an egalitarian and democratic society.

IV

SOCIAL CLASS, POLITICS AND CULTURE

THE EGALITARIAN movement which came to life in socialist clubs, trade unions, co-operative ventures and utopian communities grew stronger throughout the nineteenth century as capitalism developed. In the course of time this movement has taken many different forms—struggles for women's rights and against racial discrimination, and most recently the efforts to close the gap between rich and poor nations—but its driving force has remained the opposition to the hierarchy of social classes. The class system of the capitalist societies is seen as the very fount of inequality, from which arise the chief impediments to individual achievement and enjoyment, the major conflicts within and between nations, and the political dominance of privileged minorities.

In this movement Marx's analysis of capitalist society acquired—directly or indirectly—a large influence, through the connections which it established between social classes and political institutions. According to Marx, the upper class in society—constituted by the owners of the principal means of production—is necessarily the *ruling* class; that is, it also controls the means of political domination—legislation, the courts, the administration, military force, and the agencies of intellectual persuasion. The other classes in society, which suffer in various ways under this domination, are the source of political opposition, of new social doctrines, and eventually of a new ruling class. Only in the modern capitalist societies, however, does a situation occur in which the contending classes are reduced to two clearly demarcated groups, one of which—the working class—because it contains no significant new social divisions within itself, espouses an egalitarian creed and engages in a political struggle to bring about a classless society.

The appeal of Marx's theory is twofold: it provides a clear and inspiring formulation of the aspirations of the working class, and at the same time it offers an explanation of the development of forms of society and government, and especially of the rise of the modern labour movement itself. There are not lacking, in the present age, governments which are quite plainly the instruments of rule by an upper class, as in those economically backward countries where the landowners dominate an uneducated, unorganized and dispirited peasantry. When Marx undertook his studies the class character of governments was just as apparent in the European countries which had embarked upon industrialization. During much of the nineteenth century only property-owners in these societies enjoyed full political rights; and it was scarcely an exaggeration to conceive the government as "a committee for managing the common affairs of the *bourgeoisie* as a whole." In many European countries it was only during the first two decades of the twentieth century that universal suffrage was finally established.

Since political democracy is such a recent growth Marx can hardly be blamed for having failed to consider all its implications for the association between economic and political power. At least he did not disregard the importance of the suffrage. In an article of 1852, in which he discussed the political programme of the Chartists, he wrote:

The carrying of Universal Suffrage in England would, therefore, be a far more socialistic measure than anything which has been honoured with that name on the Continent. Its inevitable result, here, is the *political supremacy of the working class*.[1]

On a later occasion, it is true, Marx referred in a more disparaging way to the right of "deciding once in three or six years which member of the ruling class was to misrepresent the people in Parliament."[2] But he added

[1] Karl Marx, "The Chartists," *New York Daily Tribune*, August 25, 1852.
[2] *The Civil War in France* (1871).

immediately: "On the other hand, nothing could be more foreign to the spirit of the Commune than to supersede universal suffrage by hierarchic investiture." The situations which called forth these divergent assessments were in fact very different. In the one case Marx was describing a state of affairs in which a working-class movement, organized on a large scale, would be capable of putting forward its own trusted candidates at elections; while in the other he was drawing a contrast between an actual working-class government—the Commune—and a preceding condition in which the working class was able to vote only for one or another of the bourgeois parties.

The existence of large working-class parties has become a normal feature of the democratic capitalist countries, and this is one of the principal circumstances (another being the political system in the Soviet societies) which raise new problems concerning the relationship between class and politics. In a political system of this kind can the owners of property be regarded any longer as a permanent ruling class? Is the working class still a radical, revolutionary force which seeks to bring about an egalitarian society? Are the relations between classes in the political sphere still the same as they were in the nineteenth-century societies with their restricted franchise? Have new political divisions emerged alongside, or in the place of, those between classes; or have political conflicts lost some of the urgency and importance which they acquired in the period which saw the rise and growth of the labour movement? These questions lie at the heart of present controversies about the changing class structure of industrial societies.

It has become common, for example, to remark upon the great complexity of government in modern societies, and upon the influence which is exerted by the diverse interest groups which are consulted in the course of policy-making; and then to argue that where power is divided among many different groups, whose interests do not always coincide, the notion of a "ruling class" has lost all meaning. But if power is really so widely dispersed, how are we to account for the fact that the owners of property—the upper class in Marx's sense— still predominate so remarkably in government and administration, and in other elite positions; or that there has been so little redistribution of wealth and income, in spite of the strenuous and sustained effort of the labour movement to bring it about? Is it not reasonable to conclude, from the evidence provided in the last chapter, that notwithstanding political democracy, and despite the limited conflicts of interest which occur between elite groups in different spheres, the upper class in the capitalist societies is still a distinctive and largely self-perpetuating social group, and still occupies the vital positions of power? Its power may be less commanding, and it is certainly less arrogantly exer- cised, than in an earlier period, because it encounters an organized opposition and the test of elections, and because other classes have gained a limited access to the elites; but the power which it has retained enables it to defend successfully its most important economic interests.

There are other difficulties with the concept of a "ruling class," but I have examined them at length elsewhere[3] and I shall not consider them further in the present context. It is in any case the changes in the condition of the working class, and especially in its political role, which have most impressed students of class structure in the postwar period. The "new working class," it is claimed, is economically prosperous and aspires to middle-class standards of living:[4] and in consequence it has become less class conscious and less radical in politics. How far are these political inferences warranted? Class consciousness, in a broad sense, may be regarded as one form of the "consciousness of kind" which develops in all enduring social groups; for example, the consciousness of belonging to a particular nation. In this sense, the emergence of class consciousness, the increasing use of the term "class" to describe an individual's position in society, is itself a sign that new social groups have come into existence.[5] But in Marx's usage, which has had a profound influence both upon sociological theories and upon political doctrines, "class consciousness" involves something more than this; namely, the gradual formation of distinctive ideologies and political organizations which have as their object

[3] See my *Elites and Society* (New York, 1965), Chapter 2.

[4] See above, pp. 28–31.

[5] There is a good account by Asa Briggs, "The Language of 'Class' in Early Nineteenth Century England" in Asa Briggs and John Saville (eds.), *Essays in Labour History* (New York, 1960).

the promotion of particular class interests in a general conflict between classes.[6]

The growing class consciousness of the working class was represented by Marx as showing these characteristics in an exceptional degree; for it was expressed in ideologies and political movements which strongly emphasized the conflict of economic interest between capitalists and workers, and which proposed radical social changes in order to end the system of society based upon classes. The working class was, therefore, a revolutionary element in society; more revolutionary indeed than any earlier oppressed classes, since it aimed consciously at abolishing the whole class system. As Marx wrote, with youthful enthusiasm, in a sketch of his theory of modern classes which guided all his mature thinking:

A class must be formed which has *radical chains,* a class *in* civil society which is not a class *of* civil society, a class which is the dissolution of all classes, a sphere of society which has a universal character because its sufferings are universal, and which does not claim a *particular redress* because the wrong which is done to it is not a *particular wrong* but *wrong in general.* There must be formed a sphere of society which claims no *traditional* status but only a *human* status . . . a sphere finally which cannot emancipate itself without emancipating itself from all the other spheres of society, without therefore emancipating all these other spheres; which is, in short, a *total loss* of humanity and which can only redeem itself by a *total redemption of*

[6] Writing about the peasantry in *The Eighteenth Brumaire of Louis Bonaparte* Marx observed: "In so far as there is merely a local interconnection among these smallholding peasants, and the identity of their interests begets no community, no national bond, and no political organization among them, they do not form a class."

humanity. This dissolution of society, as a particular class, is the proletariat.[7]

This conception of the working class as the animator of a revolutionary movement which is to establish a classless society, appears to many sociologists to be highly questionable in the light of recent investigations. It is not that the prevalence of class consciousness in a broad sense, or the association between class membership and political affiliation, is generally denied. Social surveys have shown plainly that most people are familiar with the class structure of their society, and are aware of their own position within it. Equally, it has been shown that class membership is still the strongest single influence upon a person's social and political attitudes; and that the major political parties in most countries represent pre-eminently class interests. What is brought into question by recent studies is the view that the working class, in the advanced industrial countries, is striving to bring about a revolutionary transformation of society, rather than piecemeal reforms within the existing social structure; or that there is a total incompatibility and opposition between the doctrines and objectives of political parties which draw their main support from different classes. In Marx's theory the working class was revolutionary in two senses: first, that it aimed, or would aim, to produce the most comprehensive and fundamental change in social institutions that had ever been accomplished in

[7] Karl Marx, "Critique of Hegel's Philosophy of Right," in *Deutsch-Französische Jahrbücher* (1844).

the history of mankind, and secondly, that it would do so in the course of a sustained conflict with the *bourgeoisie* which was likely to culminate in a violent struggle for power. The nascent working class of the mid-nineteenth century fitted reasonably well into this scheme, which was constructed largely out of the experiences of the French Revolution. The "new working class" of the mid-twentieth century, it is argued, fits badly.

Studies of industrial workers during the past decade agree broadly in finding that there has been a decline in their attachment to collective ends, and so also in their enthusiasm for action as a class in order to establish a new social order. F. Zweig, in his study of workers in four modern enterprises, observes that "when speaking about classes a man would seem to be thinking primarily about himself, about the individual aspect of the problem, and not about the social situation or the social structure,"[8] and he goes on to say that although two-thirds of the workers he interviewed placed themselves in the working class, this recognition of their *class identity* was not accompanied by any strong feelings of *class allegiance*. A study of French workers[9] arrives at very similar conclusions. The authors distinguish three types of reaction among factory workers to their situation in the economy and in society: (1) evasion (the attempt to escape from industrial work

[8] F. Zweig, *The Worker in an Affluent Society* (New York, 1961), p. 134.
[9] A. Andrieux and J. Lignon, *L' Ouvrier d'aujourd'hui* (Paris, 1960).

either by rising to a higher position within the firm or by setting up in business on one's own account); (2) resignation (a dull and resentful acceptance of industrial work as an inescapable fate); and (3) revolt (opposition and resistance to the capitalist organization of industry). Of these three types, the second is by far the most common, while the third is the least so; and even the 9 per cent of workers in this category, who believe that they can improve their situation by collective action, no longer believe that any future society will be able to alter fundamentally the subordinate position of the worker in the factory. The authors summarize their results by saying that although the workers they studied still have a group consciousness (i.e. they regard themselves as "workers," clearly distinguished from other groups in the population), they no longer have any collective aims. The present-day worker is "a man who is cut off from working-class traditions and who possesses no general principles, no world-view, which might give a direction to his life."[10] This conclusion, they observe, agrees entirely with those reached in a number of studies in Germany, by Popitz, Bednarik and others. Popitz and his collaborators, in their study of workers in the Ruhr steel industry,[11] show that there is a strong working-class consciousness, which is built around the distinction between manual workers and those who plan, direct and command work;

[10] Ibid., p. 189.
[11] H. Popitz, H. P. Bahrdt, E. A. Jüres, H. Kesting, *Das Gesellschaftsbild des Arbeiters* (Tübingen, 1957).

but those who still think in Marxist terms of the victory
of the working class and the attainment of a classless
society are a small minority. Similarly, Bednarik concludes his essay on the young worker of today by saying
that "society has ceased to be an ideal for the working
class," and that the worker "tends more and more to
withdraw into private life."[12]

Several of these ideas are brought together by Goldthorpe and Lockwood, in their analysis of the notion
of *embourgeoisement*,[13] where it is suggested that there
has been, in the Western industrial countries, a con-
vergence between the "new middle class" and the "new
working class," leading to a distinctive view of society
which diverges both from the radical individualism of
the old middle classes and from the comprehensive collectivism of the old working class. In this new social
perspective collectivism is widely accepted as a means
(and this accounts for the spread of trade unionism
among white-collar workers), but no longer as an end
(which accounts for the weakening of class allegiance
among workers). Goldthorpe and Lockwood use the
terms "instrumental collectivism" and "family centred-
ness" to describe the complex of beliefs and attitudes
in this conception of society. The second term refers to
the phenomenon which other writers have described
as a withdrawal into private life, and which is revealed

[12] K. Bednarik, *Der junge Arbeiter von heute—ein neuer Typ*
(1953), pp. 138–9, 141.
[13] John H. Goldthorpe and David Lockwood, "Affluence and the
British Class Structure," *Sociological Review*, XI (2), July, 1963. See
above, pp. 30–31.

by the individual worker's predominant concern with his family's standard of living, his own prospects of advancement, the education of his children and their opportunities to enter superior occupations.

The second feature of the working class as a revolutionary force, namely its involvement in violent class struggles, can be discussed more briefly. In all the advanced industrial countries the violence of class conflict has greatly diminished over the past few decades, and the working-class parties which still regard their aims as likely to be achieved by the use of force are few in number and insignificant. The change from the conditions at the end of the nineteenth century has been produced by several factors, among which we may single out the development of political democracy, the more effective power of modern governments, aided by the great advances in military technology, in administration and in communication, and the changes in the nature of working-class aims as well as in the relations between classes. It would be a mistake to dismiss entirely the role of force in political conflicts in the Western industrial societies; for not only did violent class struggles take place as recently as the 1930s, but other types of social conflict—for example, between Negroes and whites in the USA—have often engendered violence during the past decade. Nevertheless, at the present time it is in those countries which have just embarked upon industrialization that violent struggles, especially between classes, are mainly to be found.

Changes in the relations between classes in the

capitalist societies have accompanied the changes in the character of the major social classes, influencing and being influenced by the latter. In so far as social mobility has increased, and the middle class has grown in numbers, the image of society as divided between two great contending classes has become blurred by the superimposition of another image, in which society appears as an indefinite and changing hierarchy of status positions, which merge into each other, and between which individuals and families are able to move with much greater facility than in the past. In addition, the everyday economic struggle between workers and employers has been regulated more and more by the state, through the creation of new social institutions for negotiation, arbitration and joint consultation. It is this situation which leads Ralf Dahrendorf, in his *Class and Class Conflict in Industrial Society*, to write of "post-capitalist societies" in which industrial conflicts have been institutionalized and thereby insulated from the sphere of politics; and although this is an exaggeration, inasmuch as political conflicts are still very largely about class interests, and are widely recognized as such, it contains an element of truth in so far as it points to the moderation of hostility between classes and to the emergence of political issues which are in some measure detached from questions of class interest. There is unquestionably some common ground between the main political parties in the Western industrial countries; and the development of science and technology, economic growth and rising levels of living, urban congestion and crime, are among the issues which have to be dealt with politically along much the same lines in *all* the industrial countries.

The social changes which have produced the "new working class," as well as a political climate in which violent confrontations between the classes are rare, have been interpreted by some sociologists as a crucial phase in a process which is leading to the complete assimilation of the working class into existing society, as a beginning of the "end of ideology" in the precise sense of the decline of socialist doctrines which offer a radical criticism of present-day society and the hope of an alternative form of society. But this interpretation goes beyond the facts which have been discovered by sociological research. It relies, for instance, upon a tacit comparison between the present state of working-class consciousness and its state in some vaguely located and imperfectly known past age, which is seen as a time of heroic resolution and militancy. Against this it should be observed that in the past few decades, in the very period in which the working class is supposed to have become more middle class in its outlook, the support for socialist parties in Europe has been maintained or has substantially increased. It may be objected that this support has been gained by the progressive elimination of distinctively socialist ideas from the programmes of such parties. But this too is doubtful. The language of socialism has changed over the past century, in ways which it would be rewarding to study more closely, but the ends of the labour movement—collectivism and

[89]

social equality—have not been abandoned or even seriously questioned.

The picture of working-class apathy and lack of enthusiasm for collective ends which is given by the studies mentioned earlier has to be seen, therefore, as a portrait taken at one moment of time and not as the final episode of a serial film. Even as a momentary picture it may not do justice to all the features of the situation. Serge Mallet, in his study of the "new working class" referred to above,[14] suggests that because the worker as a producer is still dominated and constrained, while as a consumer he experiences a new freedom and independence, it is in relation to the working environment that class consciousness is most vigorously expressed;[15] and this is apparent, he thinks, in the changing nature of trade-union demands in the modern sectors of industry, which are concerned increasingly with shorter hours of work, longer holidays, and greater control over the policies of management. These demands reflect the desire of the "new working class" to alter radically its position in the system of production, in a sense which is close to the ideas of classical socialist thought. The same aspirations, it may be added, find

[14] Pp. 31–32 above.

[15] This appears very clearly in the comments of workers reported in the study by Andrieux and Lignon (op. cit.). They mention frequently and bitterly the difference in the treatment which they receive from other people according to whether they are recognized as workers (in the factory, travelling to work) or as citizens (in leisure time). One worker summed it up by saying that as a worker he was pushed around, but ". . . when I am out in my car and stop to ask for directions the policeman comes up touching his cap because he thinks he is dealing with a gentleman" (pp. 31–32).

expression in the widening discussion of various forms of producers' co-operation, which has been inspired very largely by the progress of workers' self-management in Yugoslavia.

There are several other influences at work in the Western industrial societies which sustain the ideological controversies over the future form of society, and which lend support, in particular, to the socialist doctrines of the working class. One of the most important is the extension, and the more general acceptance, of public ownership of industry, public management of the economy, and public provision of a wide range of social and cultural services. The contrast between "private opulence" and "public squalor," to which J. K. Galbraith has pointed, has awakened many people to the fact that in modern societies many of the most valuable private amenities can only be got or preserved through public action. Individuals may be prosperous enough to provide adequately for their personal needs in food, housing, transport, and some kinds of entertainment, but they cannot individually assure what is needed for full enjoyment in the way of roads, facilities for sport and recreation, good working conditions, or a congenial and attractive urban environment. The unrestricted pursuit of private wealth and private enjoyment leads, indeed, to the impoverishment of these vital public services.

In the economic sphere the growth in the size of firms in major branches of industry, and the approach to monopolistic control in some sectors, has reduced the difference between the operations of publicly owned and privately owned enterprises; and if there is, at the present time, no great public excitement over the issue of "nationalization" of industry, this is in part because it is taken for granted that a change of ownership would not affect the economic performance of the industry. In part, also, it is due to recognition of the fact that the economy as a whole, in a modern society, must anyway be increasingly regulated and directed by the political authorities if a consistently high rate of growth is to be achieved, through the systematic application of science to production. Today the entrepreneur has become much less important; while the trained manager (who can perfectly well be a public servant) and the scientist have become much more important.

The increasing provision of social services by the state, which in recent times has been largely brought about by the pressure of the labour movement, has also fortified the socialist conception of a more equal, more collectivist society. Social legislation in the Welfare State may not be preponderantly egalitarian, either in intention or in effect,[16] but as it is extended and comes eventually to include an "incomes policy" so it approaches the conditions in which, as a German social scientist has observed, the task of social policy is to determine the order of priority of claims against the national product.[17] And these are conditions which

---

[16] For a discussion of this point see T. H. Marshall, *Social Policy* (New York, 1965), Chapter 13, "Retrospect and Prospect."

[17] Quoted by T. H. Marshall, *Social Policy*, p. 183.

would accord most fully with the institutions of a class-less society.

This discussion of classes and ideologies in the Western societies, if it suggests that the working class may still be considered an independent force in political life, and one which still aims to bring about radical changes in the social structure, also indicates that the development of the working class has diverged in many respects from the course which Marx and the early Marxists expected it to follow. Marx's theory dealt, necessarily, with the first stages in the formation of the working class, and it proposed broad hypotheses rather than settled conclusions based upon intensive research. The Marxist sociologists—in any case few in number—have not greatly advanced the empirical study of social classes. Often they have seemed to be writing about an imaginary society, in which a pure class struggle continues inexorably, unsullied by such events of practical life as the advent of political democracy, the extension of welfare services, the growth of national income, or the increasing governmental regulation of the economy. Marx himself, through his dramatic vision of a revolutionary confrontation between the classes and his initial optimism about the growth of the labour movement, gave some encouragement to an outlook of this kind. There had been bourgeois revolutions, therefore there would be proletarian revolutions.

Neither Marx nor his followers examined sufficiently the strengths and weaknesses of the major social classes in capitalist society, many of which, indeed, have only become apparent through the experiences of the past fifty or sixty years. Marx insisted that the ruling ideas in any society are the ideas of the ruling class. But he did not seriously consider how important the ideas themselves might be in sustaining that rule, or how difficult it would be for the working class to oppose them with its own ideas.[18] Doubtless he thought that his own social theory would have a great effect (as it has), and he also counted upon the economic failure of capitalism—the ever-worsening crises—to discredit bourgeois ideas. In fact, bourgeois ideas have only been discredited, for brief periods, in those societies which have suffered defeat in war, and it is in such circumstances that the major revolutions of the twentieth century have occurred. Otherwise it is true to say that the working class in all countries has continued to be profoundly influenced by the dominant ideas of capitalist society; for example, by nationalism and imperialism, by the competitive, acquisitive and possessive conception of human nature and social relations, and in recent times by a view of the overriding purpose of society as being the creation of ever greater material wealth. The attempts to combat these ideas reveal the immense difficulties involved in doing so. The ideal of working-class internationalism, in opposition to national rivalries

[18] Among later Marxists, Gramsci was the only one who gave much serious attention to these questions, and I should think that he was influenced in this direction by the work of his compatriot Mosca, who had introduced the term "political formula" to describe the body of doctrine which every ruling class, in his view, has to develop and to get accepted by the rest of society if it is to retain power.

and war between nations, has never been realized in more than a fragmentary form, in the face of differences of language and culture, and the manifold problems of establishing international associations at any level. On the other side, the idea of competition and of activity as mainly acquisitive easily becomes acceptable when it is associated with equality of opportunity— real or supposed—for which the working class itself has striven; while the idea of uninterrupted economic growth must clearly appeal, with reason, to those who are struggling to escape from cramping poverty.

Yet in spite of these difficulties, egalitarian and collectivist ideas have spread widely during this century. They have done so more slowly than Marx expected, but this might mean no more than that he made a mistake over the time scale while still being right about the general direction of change. The question now is whether these ideas have lost their vigour and have begun to recede, or whether they are still active and effective. A number of sociologists, as we have seen, observe a decline in the enthusiasm of the working class for collective ends, a loss of interest in any social mission, and the gradual erosion of a distinctive working-class culture. A few, among them S. M. Lipset, regard the combination of political democracy and high levels of living as the final achievement of the "good society," and thus as the terminal point of the labour movement: "democracy is not only or even primarily a means through which different groups can attain their ends or seek the good society; it is the good society itself in operation."[19] Lipset concedes that there is still a class struggle of sorts in the capitalist countries, but he sees it as being concerned only with the distribution of income, not with any profound changes in the social structure or culture; and he assumes that there is a constant trend towards greater equality of income which is turning the struggle into a process of limited bargaining between interest groups, while denuding it of all ideological or political significance.

There are several reasons to be cautious about accepting this view that the relative peace on the ideological front, and the apparent decline in the vigour of working-class social ideals, have become permanent features of the capitalist societies; that the final form of industrial society has been reached. First, it is likely that there will be growing discontent as it becomes evident that there is no general trend towards greater economic equality, and that, on the contrary, there are very powerful movements which tend to produce a more unequal distribution of income and wealth whenever the industrial and political pressure of the working class is relaxed. It is obvious, for example, that in some Western countries there is a great disproportion between the modest wage increases which many industrial workers have claimed in recent years, and the large increases of salary which some groups of professional workers have demanded. Those in the professions have many advantages in pressing their claims, especially where the supply of qualified people is limited by the

[19] S. M. Lipset, *Political Man* (New York, 1960), p. 403.

nature of the educational system; their actions are usually interpreted more sympathetically by the mass media than are the similar actions of industrial workers; and their class consciousness and determination to maintain or improve their established position in society appear to be waxing rather than waning. In society as a whole it is likely that the continued economic growth, which has benefited the working class, has brought even greater gains to those whose incomes are derived wholly or mainly from the ownership of capital. If, therefore, a tranquil and moderate struggle between classes or sectional interests, and ideological peace, depend upon a settled trend towards greater economic equality, they cannot be regarded at present as in any way assured.

A second consideration, which seems to me still more important, is that there is a growing discrepancy between the condition of the working class at work and in leisure time. Security of employment and rising levels of living have brought greater freedom of choice and independence of action for industrial workers outside the workplace, and younger workers in particular have taken advantage of their new opportunities. But one result of this is that the contrast between work and leisure has become more intense: at work there is still constraint, strict subordination, lack of responsibility, absence of means for self-expression. All the studies of the modern working class which I reviewed earlier bring out clearly that workers are profoundly aware of this division in their lives, and that they have a deep hatred of the present system of industrial work. They would undoubtedly recognize their condition in Marx's observation that a worker "does not fulfil himself in his work but denies himself, has a feeling of misery rather than well-being, does not develop freely his mental and physical powers but is physically exhausted and mentally debased," that "his work is not voluntary but imposed, *forced labour*," and that he "feels himself at home only in his leisure time."[20]

It is hard to believe that such a division can continue unchanged, but it may be overcome or mitigated in several different ways. Sustained economic growth may result in such a reduction of working hours and expansion of leisure time that the hierarchical and authoritarian structure of industry comes to play a negligible part in the individual's personal and social life, and is no longer a matter for concern. Or, on the other hand, there may be renewed efforts to introduce into the sphere of economic production some of the freedom and independence which exist in leisure time, and these efforts may be helped by changes in the character of production itself, as it becomes increasingly a scientific activity—using both the natural and the social sciences—which needs the services of highly educated and responsible individuals to carry it on. Most probably, there will be some combination of these two movements; but in so far as the second one takes place at all it will be through the actions of working-class organizations seeking to control the labour process, which

[20] Karl Marx, *Economic and Philosophical Manuscripts* (1844).

still appears, as it did to Marx, as the fundamental activity in every social system.

The rise of the working class in modern societies has been a more protracted affair than Marx supposed, and it has only rarely approached that state of decisive struggle with the *bourgeoisie* which he expected. In the future a similar gradual development appears most likely, but the end may still be Marx's ideal society, a classless society. Indeed, it is only now, when the tremendous development of the sciences has created the possibility of truly wealthy societies—but for the uncertainties of population growth and nuclear warfare—that the economic foundations of a classless society can be regarded as assured. What kinds of inequality would remain in the absence of social classes, and in conditions where individuals had independence and responsibility both at work and in leisure, can only be conjectured. There would doubtless be some differences in the prestige of occupations, in incomes, and in the social position of individuals, but there is no reason to suppose that these would be very large, or that they would be incompatible with an awareness of basic human equality and community.

The principal fault in many recent studies of social classes has been that they lack an historical sense. Like the economists of whom Marx said that they believed there had been history, because feudalism had disappeared, but there was no longer any history, because capitalism was a natural and eternal social order, some sociologists have accepted that there was an historical development of classes and of class conflicts in the early period of industrial capitalism, but that this has ceased in the fully evolved industrial societies in which the working class has escaped from poverty and has attained industrial and political citizenship. But this assumption is made without any real study of the evolution of social classes in recent times, or of the social movements at the present time which reveal the possibilities of future social change. An historical analysis of the changing class structure in modern societies, such as I have merely outlined here, remains one of the most important unfulfilled tasks of sociology today.

POSTSCRIPT
TO THE AMERICAN
EDITION

POSTSCRIPT TO
THE AMERICAN
EDITION

THE DISTINCTIVE character of the American class system
has been recognized by social thinkers at least since the
time of de Tocqueville. Early in the present century a
German economist and historian, Werner Sombart, published an essay[1] in which he sought to account for the
absence of socialism—that is, of a class-conscious working-
class movement—in the United States, and found an answer
mainly in the high degree of mobility between the classes.
Some fifty years later a Polish sociologist, Stanislaw Ossowski, examining the phenomenon which he called "non-egali-
tarian classlessness" in America, concluded that the most
important element in the view of those numerous Americans
who see their society as "classless" is the idea that there
are no distinct and insuperable barriers between the various
strata of society.[2] In the present book I have discussed
the same question in the course of a comparison between
the United States and some European countries. But I have
done so very briefly, and the publication of an American
edition affords an opportunity and a possible justification
for examining more fully this ideological and political classlessness, as well as those recent social trends—the Negro

[1] Werner Sombart, *Warum gibt es in den Vereinigten Staaten keinen
Sozialismus?* (1906).
[2] Stanislaw Ossowski, *Class Structure in the Social Consciousness*
(New York, Free Press of Glencoe, Inc., 1963), pp. 100–10.

[103]

revolt, the rediscovery of poverty amidst prosperity, the revival of radical criticism—which may change profoundly the political outlook.

Two books, published with an interval of nearly twenty years, give an excellent view of the changing conceptions of social class among American social scientists, and at the same time suggest a relationship between these conceptions and the condition of American society. Charles H. Page, in his *Class and American Sociology: From Ward to-Ross*,[3] shows how the founders of American academic sociology reacted against the individualistic theory of Herbert Spencer, which had had so great an influence upon American social thought, and how they introduced in their writings the ideas of class and class struggle. These ideas were taken in large measure from the work of German historians and sociologists, but they were at the same time a response to the changing American society of the closing decades of the nineteenth century, when the great trusts came into existence, the tide of social criticism mounted, and labour organizations on the European model began to be formed. Of the writers whose work Professor Page discusses, Sumner, in particular, was still a defender of the *status quo*, but he felt obliged nonetheless to confront the problem of class interests, and in his book *What Social Classes Owe to Each Other* he expounded, as an answer to the evident tensions in American society, a doctrine of social harmony based upon the idea of the mutual dependence of the major classes. Others among the early sociologists, and notably Small, Ward and Ross, became much more critical of the economic inequality and the imperfect democracy of their society, and their radicalism became manifest in the importance which they attributed to the divergence of class interests. In the writings of Albion Small, who was influenced both by Marx and by Gumplowicz, the theme of class conflict occupies a large place, as it did later in the

[3] Published 1940; reprinted 1964 by Octagon House, Inc., New York.

work of Veblen, though at this stage the classes had ceased to be those of Marx.

The interest of Professor Page's book is not only that it draws attention to the deep concern of the fathers of American sociology with the class structure of their society in its political bearing, but that it was written at a time when this concern had revived very strongly as an accompaniment of the economic depression and the intensification of class struggles and ideological conflicts in all the great industrial countries. The book appeared, however, just at the close of that era, when American society was about to enter a period of sustained economic growth and more general prosperity. In the next two decades the study of social stratification took quite a different turn, as Leonard Reissman's survey, *Class in American Society*,[4] makes plain. Instead of the opposition between major classes in a political struggle it was now the manifestations of social prestige in the local community, evaluated in terms of consumption patterns and styles of life, or occupational prestige and individual mobility through the educational system, which absorbed the attention of sociologists. The underlying conception was that of America as a middle-class society in which some people were simply more middle class than others.

The sociologists' view received support from observers of the political scene. Professor Hofstadter, for instance, in two articles on conservatism in America,[5] makes a distinction between "class politics" and "status politics" in order to account for the differences between the political movements of the 1930s and those of the 1950s, and argues that whereas "class politics" predominate in times of economic depression and discontent, "status politics" come to the fore in periods of prosperity. This argument is meant to have a general application, but Professor Hofstadter thinks that in the

[4] New York, Free Press of Glencoe, Inc., 1959.

[5] Richard Hofstadter, "The Pseudo-Conservative Revolt" and "Pseudo-Conservatism Revisited: A Postscript" in Daniel Bell, ed., *The Radical Right* (New York, Doubleday & Co., Inc., 1963), pp. 75–95, 97–103.

United States the basis for "status politics" is broader and stronger than elsewhere because of "the rootlessness and heterogeneity of American life, and above all, of its peculiar scramble for status and its peculiar search for secure identity."[6] The scramble and the search are explained in turn by the massive immigration between 1881 and 1920, which exacerbated the struggle to "belong," to acquire or retain a recognized status. Even struggles of this kind, however, may have a realistic character in periods of economic hardship and may issue in programs of social reform; but in prosperous times they are likely to run riot and to project into the political arena "utterly irrelevant fantasies and disorders of a purely personal kind."[7] In the second of his articles Professor Hofstadter extends the notion of "status politics" to comprehend what he calls "cultural politics," or the persistence of specific historical themes in the political life of a given society. This draws attention to an important element in politics, but it opens up a range of problems different from those indicated by the contrast between "class politics" and "status politics," which refers not so much to the variations between societies as to the temporal fluctuations in political activity in the modern industrial societies taken as a whole.

This conception of the alternation of "class politics" and "status politics," which makes use in a somewhat different sense of an idea of Max Weber's,[8] is open to criticism. In

[6] *Ibid.*, p. 83.

[7] *Ibid.*, p. 100.

[8] "When the bases of the acquisition and distribution of goods are relatively stable, stratification by status is favored. Every technological repercussion and economic transformation threatens stratification by status and pushes the class situation into the foreground. Epochs and countries in which the naked class situation is of predominant significance are regularly the periods of economic and technological transformations." Max Weber, "Classes, Status Groups and Parties," translated in H. H. Gerth and C. Wright Mills, eds., *From Max Weber: Essays in Sociology* (New York, Oxford University Press, 1946) pp. 193–94.

the European societies of the twentieth century, class has generally been a predominant factor in politics and remains so at the present time, but "status politics" have always had a place, particularly in the social outlook of the middle classes. There were, for example, plenty of "irrelevant fantasies and disorders" of a personal kind in German politics of the period which saw the rise to power of the National Socialists, even though the major political struggle was one between social classes. In the United States, on the other hand, it seems true to say that "status politics" have always predominated since the early years of this century, if only because one of the protagonists in a confrontation between classes—namely, the working class—has always been absent as an organized and ideologically committed force. Among the reasons for this, in addition to those which are habitually adduced, such as American individualism and the opportunities for social mobility, may be counted the ethnic diversity of American industrial workers in the crucial period from 1880 to 1920, and the pressures of national sentiment in a "new nation." The United States has exhibited in microcosm the difficulties which prevented the workers of the world from uniting effectively, and at the same time has shown the power of a national community to subdue class hostilities.

The consequences of this absence are plain. As there was no labour movement in which socialist doctrines and trade union organizations became firmly allied, so there were never any "class politics" strong enough or independent enough to supply an alternative to the "status politics" which arose from the need to belong or from such historical oppositions as those between North and South, or between the states and the federal authority. There have been radical movements among intellectuals (including social scientists), and it is this which makes plausible the contrast between the politics of the 1930s and those of the 1950s, but such movements have never influenced more than a small part of the working class. The revival of intellectual radicalism in the 1960s, which is unusual and perhaps surprising insofar as it is occurring in a period of economic prosperity, poses the question whether there are changes taking place in the United States which will in the future induce or encourage the formation of a working-class political movement.

This same question may be put in another way by asking, as Mrs. Joan Robinson once did, whether capitalism can survive in a single country—namely, in the United States. I shall not pretend to answer the question adequately in the brief compass of a postscript, but I shall try to set out the important elements of an answer. First of all, the present intellectual radicalism has the advantage of being linked with a practical and realistic political movement, that of the American Negroes for economic, civil and political rights. This movement is not a class struggle, as I have observed in the book, because it does not aim at the present time to bring about any radical changes in the form of American society, only to secure a decent place for the Negro within it. Nevertheless, the Negro revolt has provoked, in the civil rights movement, a fundamental questioning of the nature of American society, and it has been at least partly responsible for the present concern with poverty, urban slums, and other social problems. As the revolt proceeds, and if it results, for example, in the greater unionization of Negro workers, it may bring about changes in the ideology of the American working class which will be favourable to the emergence of a more radical labour movement. The acceptance of the Negro in American society is only one aspect of a more general process. As the era of mass immigration recedes—and it is already nearly two generations away—so the importance of ethnic divisions must be expected to decline. It follows from this that the bases of "status politics" are likely to be gradually eroded and the conditions created in which class interests are more clearly perceived. This is a phenomenon which it would be exciting and useful for sociologists to investigate in the next decade.

A second factor to be considered is the changing balance of social ideals in the modern world. In much of Europe and in most of the third world socialist doctrines have become predominant, and the United States can hardly escape their influence. Indeed, this influence is plainly to be seen in the notion of the 'Great Society'—now officially proclaimed as the goal of the American people—which although it harks back to the New Deal is essentially a reflection of the European "Welfare State." It is still a pale reflection; yet even in its present form it diverges widely from traditional American ideals of individualism, self-help, free enterprise and minimum government; and it is bitterly assailed by conservative thinkers on these grounds. However, if an external model is to influence a society in this fashion there must be some propitious circumstances within the receiving society. In the United States I think that the circumstances are to be found in a growing hostility to the culture of capitalism, as Schumpeter once suggested. Capitalism may deliver the goods economically speaking, though we now know that a planned economy is able to do so just as effectively. What capitalism, at least in its extreme individualistic and enterprising form, cannot do is to produce a civilized society, because it gives an excessive importance to sentiments and modes of activity—material production, acquisitiveness, competitiveness—which need to be restrained if civilization is to flourish. According to Schumpeter it was the modern secular intellectuals who initiated the moral hostility to capitalism, and he might have cited as an instance even such a moderate thinker as J. S. Mill, who wrote in his *Principles of Political Economy:* "I confess I am not charmed with the ideal of life held out by those who think that the normal state of human beings is that of struggling to get on; that the trampling, crushing, elbowing, and treading on each other's heels, which form the existing type of social life, are the most desirable lot of human kind, or anything but the disagreeable symptoms of one of the phases of industrial progress."

Is anyone charmed any longer? The disaffection of the

intellectuals has continued and even increased in recent times; but more important is the fact that the hostility to the culture of capitalism seems to have spread far beyond the confines of this small group. Concern about public squalor, the ugliness and inhumanity of the great cities, the standards of public education, and the influence of the mass media, added to the concern about poverty and inequality of rights, has begun to affect the social attitudes of a large proportion of the population. How far this readiness to accept fundamental changes in American society has gone it is impossible to determine exactly on present evidence, but it can scarcely be doubted that the new attitudes are widely diffused, since it is they which sustain the social policies of the Great Society.

Even if it be accepted, however, that there is now in the United States a form of social conflict—the Negro revolt—which anticipates in some degree a more general opposition of class interests, and an intellectual radical movement which has wide repercussions, it may still be doubted whether these will ever culminate in a working-class, socialist movement. One obvious impediment is that, just as in the past, the American trade unions have remained largely untouched by the new radicalism. Until they are affected, until a class consciousness emerges in these organized groups of the working class, there can be no effective socialist politics. It may well be too late for anything of the kind to occur. The growth of the middle classes and increasing prosperity, which have moderated class ideologies in the European countries, may still prevent their appearance at all in the United States. On the other hand, present social conflicts, the extension of automation, the declining role of the entrepreneur, the enormous social problems of the 1960s, the evident uncertainty about the quality of the American way of life, the impact of socialist ideas in the rest of the world, may produce the opposite result. But even supposing that a more widely based radical movement began to develop, how could it ever find a place, or achieve success, in the established two-party system? It is true that the obstacles confronting a nascent third party are formidable. Nevertheless, such parties have been successful, and the British Labour Party is one example. More apposite and interesting, perhaps, is the case of the New Democratic Party in Canada, since it is both recent and North American. The NDP has succeeded in establishing itself as a major party during a period of remarkable economic prosperity, and in the recent general election it increased substantially its share of the votes. It resembles the British Labour Party in that it receives the direct support of trade unions, and achieves, though on a smaller scale, that association between radical intellectuals and the industrially organized working class which is an essential condition for the success of a socialist movement.

How far this experience may be relevant to the present conditions in the United States has still to be seen. There are signs, I think, that a new political movement may develop successfully over the next few decades. In my view, this will be essential for the accomplishment of any great social reforms in the United States, and even for the preservation of the liberal and democratic character of American society.

BIBLIOGRAPHY

Selected Bibliography

General Works

Aron, Raymond, *La Lutte de classes* (Paris, Gallimard, 1964).

Dahrendorf, Ralf, *Class and Class Conflict in Industrial Society* (Stanford, Cal., Stanford University Press, 1959).

Djilas, Milovan, *The New Class* (New York, Frederick A. Praeger, Inc., 1957).

Geiger, Theodor, *Die Klassengesellschaft im Schmelztiegel* (Köln-Hagen, 1949).

International Sociological Association, *Transactions of the Third World Congress of Sociology* (London, 1956), Vol. III.

Marshall, T. H., *Class, Citizenship and Social Development* (Garden City, N.Y., Doubleday & Co., Inc., 1964). (Published in England as *Sociology at the Crossroads and Other Essays.*)

Ossowski, Stanislaw, *Class Structure in the Social Consciousness* (New York, Free Press of Glencoe, Inc., 1963).

Schumpeter, J. A., "Social Classes in an Ethnically Homogeneous Environment," in *Imperialism and Social Classes* (New York, Meridian Books, 1955).

Weber, Max, "Class, Status, Party," in H. H. Gerth and C. Wright Mills, eds., *From Max Weber: Essays in Sociology* (New York, Oxford University Press, 1946).

The Upper Classes

Aron, Raymond, "Classe sociale, classe politique, classe dirigeante," *European Journal of Sociology*, I (2), 1960, pp. 260–82.

Baltzell, E. Digby, *An American Business Aristocracy* (New York, Collier Books, 1962).

Bottomore, T. B., *Elites and Society* (New York, Basic Books, Inc., Publishers, 1965), Chap. 2.

Guttsman, W. L., *The British Political Elite* (New York, Basic Books, Inc., Publishers, 1964.).

Meisel, James H., *The Myth of the Ruling Class: Gaetano Mosca and the Elite* (Ann Arbor, University of Michigan Press, 1958).

Mills, C. Wright, *The Power Elite* (New York, Oxford University Press, 1956).

Mosca, Gaetano, *The Ruling Class* (New York, McGraw-Hill Book Company, 1939).

Veblen, Thorstein, *The Theory of the Leisure Class* (1899; new edition, New York, Mentor Books, 1953, with an introduction by C. Wright Mills).

The Middle Classes

Croner, Fritz, *Soziologie der Angestellten* (Köln, Berlin, Kiepenheuer and Witsch, 1962).

Crozier, Michel, "Classes sans conscience ou préfiguration de la société sans classes," *European Journal of Sociology*, I (2), 1960, pp. 233–47.

Inventaires III. Classes moyennes (Paris, Félix Alcan, 1939).

Lockwood, David, *Blackcoated Worker* (New York, Oxford University Press, 1958).

Mills, C. Wright, *White Collar: The American Middle Classes* (New York, Oxford University Press, 1951).

The Working Class

Andrieux, Andrée, and Lignon, Jean, *L'Ouvrier d'aujourd'hui* (Paris, Marcel Rivière, 1960).

Blauner, Robert, *Alienation and Freedom: The Factory Worker and His Industry* (Chicago, University of Chicago Press, 1964).

Briefs, G. A., *The Proletariat* (New York, McGraw-Hill Book Company, 1937).

Goldthorpe, John H., and Lockwood, David, "Affluence and the British Class Structure," *The Sociological Review*, XI (2), July 1963, pp. 133–63).

Hoggart, Richard, *The Uses of Literacy* (New York, Oxford University Press, 1957).

Lockwood, David, "The 'New Working Class,'" *European Journal of Sociology*, I (2), 1960, pp. 248–59.

Mallet, Serge, *La Nouvelle Classe ouvrière* (Paris, Editions du Seuil, 1963).

Popitz, H., Bahrdt, H. P., Jüres, E. A., and Kesting, H., *Das Gesellschaftsbild des Arbeiters* (Tübingen, J. C. B. Mohr, 1957).

Thompson, E. P., *The Making of the English Working Class* (New York, Pantheon Books, 1964).

Zweig, Ferdynand, *The Worker in an Affluent Society* (New York, Free Press of Glencoe, Inc., 1962).

Class Consciousness

Halbwachs, Maurice, *The Psychology of Social Class* (New York, Free Press of Glencoe, Inc., 1959).

Centers, Richard, *The Psychology of Social Classes* (Princeton, Princeton University Press, 1949).

Lukàcs, Georg, *Geschichte und Klassenbewusstsein* (Berlin, Malik Verlag, 1923). French translation, *Histoire et conscience de classe* (Paris, Editions de Minuit, 1960).

Mannheim, Karl, "Conservative Thought," in *Essays on Sociology and Social Psychology* (New York, Oxford University Press, 1953).

Class Conflict, Social Revolution

Arendt, Hannah, *On Revolution* (New York, The Viking Press, Inc., 1965).

Dahrendorf, Ralf, "Über einige Probleme der soziologischen Theorie der Revolution," *European Journal of Sociology*, II (1), 1961, pp. 153–62.

Geiger, Theodor, *Die Masse und ihre Aktion: ein Beitrag zur Soziologie der Revolution* (Stuttgart, F. Enke, 1926).

Geiger, Theodor, "Revolution," in A. Vierkandt (ed.), *Handwörterbuch der Soziologie* (Stuttgart, F. Enke, 1931), pp. 511–18.

Kautsky, Karl, *The Social Revolution* (Chicago, C. H. Kerr & Co., 1903).

Meusel, A., "Revolution and Counter-revolution," in *Encyclopedia of the Social Sciences* (New York, McGraw-Hill Book Company, 1934), Vol. XIII, pp. 367–76.

Sorel, Georges, *Reflections on Violence* (New York, Free Press of Glencoe, Inc., 1950).

See also the books by Aron and Dahrendorf mentioned under "General Works" above.

. . .

Social Mobility

Carlsson, Gösta, *Social Mobility and Class Structure* (Lund, Sweden, Gleerup, 1958).

Floud, J. E., Halsey, A. H., and Martin, F. M., *Social Class and Educational Opportunity* (London, William Heinemann, Ltd., 1957).

Girard, Alain, *La Réussite sociale en France* (Paris, Presses Universitaires de France, 1961).

Glass, D. V. (ed.), *Social Mobility in Britain* (New York, Free Press of Glencoe, Inc., 1955).

Lipset, S. M., and Bendix, R., *Social Mobility in Industrial Society* (Berkeley, University of California Press, 1959).

Miller, S. M., "Comparative Social Mobility," *Current Sociology*, IX (1), 1960.

Sorokin, P. A., *Social Mobility* (New York, 1927); reprinted with a chapter from his *Social and Cultural Dynamics* (New York, Free Press of Glencoe, Inc., 1959).

Index